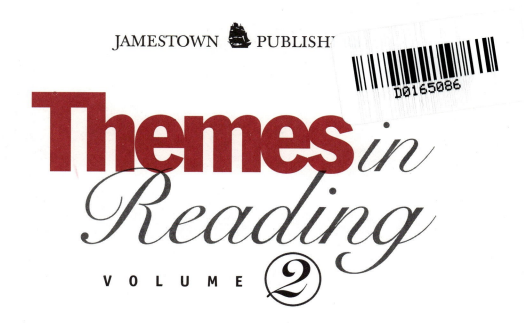

JAMESTOWN PUBLISH

D0165086

Themes *in* Reading

VOLUME ②

A MULTICULTURAL COLLECTION

JAMESTOWN PUBLISHERS

A DIVISION OF NTC/CONTEMPORARY
PUBLISHING COMPANY

Manufactured in the United States of America
International Standard Book Number: 0-89061-812-7
10 9 8 7 6 5 4 3 2 1

Executive Editor
Marilyn Cunningham

Editorial
Michael Carpenter
Paulinda Lynk
Bernice Rappaport

Permissions
Doris Milligan

Production and Design
PiperStudiosInc

Illustrations
Jason O'Malley

Contents

Unit 2: Families

Unit 3: Memories

Unit 4: Surprises

Turning Points

A turning point is a change so important that everything after that time is very different than it was before. Turning points in history change countries and civilizations. Personal turning points change the course of people's lives.

A turning point may occur because a person decides to make a change, such as moving to a new city or getting married. Often, though, people have no control over events that mark turning points in their lives. Whether planned or

unplanned, turning points cause people to make choices that affect their futures.

As the selections in this unit illustrate, a person may not even realize at the time that a turning point has occurred.

Think about some turning points in your life. How did they affect you? How was your life different after each one?

Clemente at Bat

Paul Robert Walker

The road to becoming a major-league baseball player can take many twists and turns. How does Roberto Clemente show he's up to the challenge?

l Campanis stood on the playing field at Sixto Escobar Stadium and looked at the semicircle of eager young men waiting for his instructions. Many of them were still teenagers, standing nervously in the baggy uniforms of local amateur teams. There were 72 in all. And every one of them wanted to be a big-league ballplayer.

"All right," Campanis said, "you all know why you're here. Señor Zorilla and the Santurce baseball club have been kind enough to invite me down here to take a look. There's no reason to be nervous. Just do your best and show me what you've got."

Campanis was a scout for the Brooklyn Dodgers. For the past three years, he'd been traveling to Puerto Rico, Cuba, and the Dominican Republic looking for talented players. It was 1952, and American baseball was changing. Five years earlier, Jackie Robinson had become the first black man to play on a major-league team. In 1951, a black player from Cuba named Minnie Minoso starred for the

Chicago White Sox. Suddenly, the dark-skinned boys of the Puerto Rican barrios[1] had a reason to dream.

"Everybody in the outfield," Campanis ordered. "I want to see you throw to the plate."

As the boys jogged out into center field, Campanis took his position in foul territory. Beside him was a coach with a clipboard. Each of the boys wore a number pinned to the back of his shirt. On the coach's clipboard was a list of their names and numbers.

Campanis watched as boy after boy launched long lobs from deep center field. These local tryouts were usually a waste of time. Still, he thought, you never know. Suddenly one of the boys caught his attention. A skinny kid leaned back in deep center field and fired a perfect strike to the plate. Al Campanis could hardly believe his eyes.

"Uno más!"[2] he shouted.

Once again, the boy cocked his right arm and fired. The ball flew on a perfect line and smacked the hard leather of the catcher's glove.

"Who is that kid?" Campanis asked.

The coach standing beside him looked at the number on the boy's back and compared it with the list on his clipboard. "Clemente," he said. "Roberto Clemente."

When all the boys had taken their throws, Mr. Campanis took out his stopwatch and timed them in the 60-yard dash. The world's record was 6.1 seconds. In his full baseball uniform, Roberto ran the distance in 6.4 seconds. Once again, Al Campanis could not believe his eyes.

"Uno más," he said. Roberto walked back to the starting line and ran again. Campanis stared at the stopwatch in amazement—6.4 seconds twice in a row.

"Thank you, gentlemen," Campanis said to the rest of the boys. "You may go. Clemente, I want to see you hit."

Roberto stepped into the batting cage. Campanis watched as the skinny kid in the baggy uniform smashed line drives all over the field. After a few minutes, the scout noticed that Roberto was standing too far from the plate. He ordered the pitcher to keep the ball outside.

The way he's standing, Campanis thought, he'll never be able to reach it.

The pitcher leaned back and fired a high outside fastball. Roberto swung with both feet off the ground and smashed the ball up the middle.

"What do you think?"

Al Campanis turned to look at the man who had spoken. It was Señor Marín, the man who had first discovered Roberto's talent. Both Campanis and Marín knew that Roberto was major-league material. But Campanis did his best to hide his excitement. Roberto was still in high school, and the Dodgers could not yet legally sign him to a contract.

"He has great tools," Campanis said, "but he needs polish."

"Caramba! What a pair of hands!" Pedrín Zorilla eyed the skinny, quiet boy standing in the living room of

Zorilla's beachfront home in the town of Manatí. It was a few months after the tryout in Sixto Escobar Stadium. Roberto Clemente had just turned eighteen.

"I tell you, Pedrín, he's a gem. An unpolished gem," said Señor Marín.

Zorilla continued to stare at Roberto's hands. Zorilla was the owner of the Santurce Crabbers, one of the top teams in the Puerto Rican winter league. He had seen many great ballplayers in his time, but he had never seen a young boy with such long, powerful fingers.

"Shots, Pedrín. You remember the tryout. He hit nothing but line shots."

Zorilla looked at his friend, Señor Marín. Then he looked again at Roberto Clemente. "A tryout is one thing," he said. "A game is another. I would like to see him play."

A few days later, Pedrín Zorilla watched Roberto in action with the Ferdinand Juncos team in the Puerto Rican amateur league. In the second inning, Roberto knocked in two runs with a long double. Two innings later, he followed with a 400-foot triple. In the seventh, he smashed another double. In the top of the ninth, his perfect throw from center field nailed a runner at the plate.

"Well, Marín," said Señor Zorilla, "we can give him a $400 bonus and maybe $40.00 a week until he learns to wear a uniform."

Roberto sat silently on Señor Zorilla's flagstone patio. It was a warm sunny day, and a fresh breeze was blowing off the Atlantic. Although he listened respectfully as the two older men discussed his contract, inside Roberto was bubbling over with excitement. A professional baseball player! He could hardly believe his ears.

"What should I do?" Roberto asked as Señor Marín drove him to Barrio San Antón. "What should I do?"

The older man watched the road ahead as he considered Roberto's question. It had been three years since he first saw Roberto hitting tin cans in Barrio San Antón. He had done his best to help the young boy develop his natural talent. He drove him to and from the games. He praised him when he played well, and he encouraged him when he did not. He cared for Roberto as if he were his own son. But this was a decision he did not have the right to make.

"We'll discuss it with your father," he said finally. "We'll talk it over, and he'll decide."

That evening, Don Melchor looked over the piece of paper in his hand. "Very interesting," he said. "I must think about this." Don Melchor showed Roberto's contract to one of his neighbors. "They are offering Roberto $400 to play baseball," he said.

During his many years of hard work in the sugar fields, Don Melchor had never found time to learn how to read. He listened carefully as the neighbor read the whole contract out loud. "What do you think?" he asked.

"When they offer $400," the neighbor replied, "it means he is worth much more. Don't sign a thing."

The next day, Don Melchor and Señor Marín went to the house of Pedrín Zorilla. Don Melchor looked around the beautiful living room. There are many fine things in this house, he thought. This Señor Zorilla is a wealthy man.

"I think you can give more money for my boy," said Don Melchor. "He is a fine player."

Pedrín Zorilla looked at the wiry black man who stood before him. Don Melchor Clemente was 71 years old, but he had the strength of a much younger man. Zorilla admired Don Melchor's faith in the talents of his son. But he also knew that $400 was a good bonus for a Puerto Rican player. Many boys signed for $100 or less.

"Frankly," said Señor Zorilla, "if you want more money, I have no interest in him. I think he's good, but he's got no record to prove it."

That night, the Clemente family sat around the dinner table. They were all very excited about Roberto's chance to play professional baseball. "Don't worry," Don Melchor said. "They will offer more. We will just have to wait."

Roberto stared down at the roast pork on his plate. He did not feel very hungry. All his life he had dreamed about playing professional baseball. Now he was offered a chance. What difference did a few dollars make? Slowly, he looked up from the plate and directly into his father's eyes.

"Papá," he said, "I don't want to wait. I want to play."

Don Melchor stared at Roberto. In eighteen years, his youngest son had never spoken to him like this. It was always, "Yes, Papá" or "Your blessing, Papá."

For a moment, Don Melchor was angry. "What do you mean you do not want to wait? If I say you wait, then you wait."

"But, Papá," Roberto replied, "you always say a man must work for what he needs. Their offer is fair. When I prove myself, then they will pay me more."

Don Melchor silently considered Roberto's words. No, he thought, there is no reason for anger. Roberto has learned his lessons well. It is good for a boy to become a man.

"All right," he said seriously, "tell the man I will sign."

Roberto sat on the hard wooden bench and held his head in his hands. The Santurce Crabbers were playing the team from Ponce, a city in the south of Puerto Rico. The Crabbers were leading 7–5 in the bottom of the eighth inning, but Roberto was not very happy. It was already two months into the season, and so far he had only played in a few games as a pinch hitter or a late-inning defensive[3] replacement.

[3] the type of sports player whose job is to prevent the opposite team from scoring

If this is professional baseball, Roberto thought, I would be better off buying a ticket and watching it from the grandstand. At least there I'd have a comfortable seat.

Santurce had many fine players from the major leagues. The Puerto Rican fans take their baseball very seriously, and Santurce was fighting for the league championship. There was not much opportunity for an eighteen-year-old rookie who was still in high school. But this didn't make Roberto feel any better. He was good at playing baseball. He was not very good at sitting on the bench.

That night, Roberto spoke to Señor Marín as he drove him home from the game. "If I don't play tomorrow," he said, "I quit."

"Chico!" said Señor Marín, "what are you talking about?"

"I mean it," said Roberto. "I am here to play, not to sit."

"Hmmmm," said Señor Marín. "I will speak to Señor Zorilla."

"The young one wants to play."

"You know how I feel about rookies," said Pedrín Zorilla. "We have many great pitchers in this league. I tell you, Marín, a boy like Clemente strikes out three or four times in a row and suddenly he starts asking questions. 'Can I hit? Can I really play?' It is important he does not give himself the wrong answers."

"But the boy is desperate,"[4] said Señor Marín. "You cannot keep him on the bench."

[4] has little or no hope

"Listen, Marín," said Señor Zorilla. "I am the man who pays his salary. Clemente plays when I say he plays."

That night, Señor Marín drove Roberto to the ballpark. "Take it easy, Chico," said the older man. "Your day will come. Señor Zorilla says he will play you soon."

"You're dragging your left foot. You're bailing out. That's OK for the inside pitches, but you'll never be able to hit the outside curveball."

Roberto listened carefully to his manager, Buster Clarkson. Clarkson was a husky shortstop who had been a great star in the Negro Leagues. He had just finished his only major-league season with the Boston Braves. Now he was playing and managing with the Santurce Crabbers.

"Here, let's try this." Clarkson laid a bat on the ground behind Roberto's feet. "Now I want you to swing without touching the bat with your left foot." Clarkson nodded to the pitcher. "Nothing but outside curves," he shouted.

For twenty minutes, Roberto stood in the batter's box and practiced hitting the outside curveballs without dragging his left foot. At first, it was very difficult. Ever since he was a small boy in Barrio San Antón, he had dragged his left foot away from the pitch. But this was not a guava stick in his hands, and the pitchers in the Puerto Rican winter league did not throw a big ball of rags.

"That's it," said Clarkson, "step right into the pitch." The veteran player watched as Roberto struggled to adjust his batting style. Soon the skinny eighteen-year-old was smashing the outside curveball for line drives to right and center field.

"Now you've got it," Clarkson said. "Keep it up and you'll be as good as Willie Mays."

When Roberto was finished with batting practice, Clarkson watched the young player run smoothly toward the outfield. He turned to the coach beside him and smiled. "That kid's gonna be all right," he said. "He listens, he works hard, and he doesn't make the same mistake twice."

Late in the season, the Santurce Crabbers were playing in Caguas. It was the top of the ninth inning, and the Crabbers had the bases loaded with two outs. Santurce was down by two runs. This was their last chance.

The next man up was Bob Thurman. Thurman was a solid batter who later played in the major leagues, but he had trouble hitting left-handed pitchers and Caguas had a lefty on the mound. Buster Clarkson called Thurman back from the on-deck circle and looked down the bench at Clemente. "Grab yourself a bat," he said.

As Roberto stepped up to the plate, he looked around the stadium. There were thousands of fans in the stands. Although it was night, the field was as bright as the middle of the day. Roberto thought for a moment of the muddy field in Barrio San Antón. Then he stepped into the batter's box.

He took two level practice swings, cocked his bat, and waited for the pitch. The white ball came toward him in a blur. It was not in slow motion as he had imagined when he was a boy. It was fast. Very fast. Roberto swung wildly and missed.

Roberto took a deep breath and set himself for the next pitch. This time he was ready. With a powerful flick of his wrists, he reached out and smashed the ball down the right-field line. He rounded first base at full speed and slid into second with a double. All three runs scored. Santurce had taken the lead.

From then on, Roberto was given more and more chances to play. The next year, in his second season with the Crabbers, he broke into the starting lineup. Roberto thrilled the Puerto Rican fans with his dazzling catches and powerful arm in right field, and he batted a solid .288 in the lead-off spot. The great tools that Al Campanis had seen in the tryout at Sixto Escobar Stadium were gradually becoming polished to major-league quality.

Epilogue

Clemente, drafted at twenty-one by the Pittsburgh Pirates, spent his entire major-league career with them. He got his 3,000th major-league hit at the end of the 1972 season. Unfortunately, Clemente's life ended that year, on New Year's Eve. He was killed in a plane crash on his way to deliver relief supplies to the victims of an earthquake in Nicaragua. Clemente was elected to the Baseball Hall of Fame in 1973.

About the Author

Paul Robert Walker has written more than a dozen books for young people. This excerpt is from *Pride of Puerto Rico: the Life of Roberto Clemente*. Among the groups that have honored Walker's works are the American Folklore Society and the Council for Social Studies. In addition to writing, Walker has worked as a high school literature teacher.

Responding to the Biography

▼ Think Back

Why were Roberto and the other young men especially hopeful and excited about the baseball tryouts?

Why does Roberto's father think $400 is not enough money for Roberto's contract? Why do Roberto and Pedrín Zorilla think it is a fair amount?

Why did Señor Zorilla not want to play Roberto and other rookies?

▼ Discuss

Roberto was eighteen when he was offered the professional baseball contract. Yet the final decision to sign was made by his father. At what age should a person be able to make important decisions? Why?

Do you think Roberto was right to demand playing time with a threat to quit? What would you have done? Explain.

▼ Write

Write Character Sketches After reading this biographical excerpt, you should have a good idea of what Roberto Clemente, his father Don Melchor, and Señor Zorilla were like. Write three short character sketches describing their personalities.

Write a Tribute Think about someone you admire. What qualities does that person have? Write a character sketch telling about that person and the special qualities you admire about her or him.

Fifteen

William Stafford

Notice how admiringly this teenager describes his discovery. He wishes that finders could be keepers.

South of the bridge on Seventeenth

I found back of the willows one summer

day a motorcycle with engine running

as it lay on its side, ticking over

slowly in the high grass. I was fifteen.

I admired all the pulsing gleam, the

shiny flanks,[1] the demure[2] headlights

fringed where it lay; I led it gently

to the road and stood with that

companion, ready and friendly. I was fifteen.

[1] sides

[2] shy

We could find the end of a road, meet

the sky out on Seventeenth. I thought about

hills, and patting the handle got back a

confident opinion. On the bridge we indulged[3]   [3] gave in to

a forward feeling, a tremble. I was fifteen.

Thinking, back farther in the grass I found

the owner, just coming to, where he had flipped

over the rail. He had blood on his hand, was pale—

I helped him walk to his machine. He ran his hand

over it, called me good man, roared away.

I stood there, fifteen.

About the Author

William Stafford (1914–1993) was born and educated in Kansas and taught literature for thirty years at Lewis and Clark College in Portland, Oregon. He won many awards for his prose and poetry. Most of his poems take place on a mountainside, a riverbank, or a roadside, or as Stafford himself said, "near an exit." In an interview about his writing, he also said, "I feel very exploratory when I write. . . . I feel like Daniel Boone going into Kentucky."

Responding to the Poem

▼ Think Back

The speaker finds a motorcycle lying on its side in the grass. How did it get there? What happened before the speaker came along?

Does the speaker want to take the motorcycle? How can you tell?

At what point does the speaker change his mind about taking the motorcycle? What do his actions tell you about him?

▼ Discuss

In your opinion, why does William Stafford repeat the phrase "I was fifteen"?

In what ways would the poem be different if the speaker had been seven or twenty-seven instead of fifteen?

▼ Write

Use Personification Stafford uses personification—giving human qualities to nonhuman things—to describe the motorcycle. Write a short descriptive paragraph, using personification, about something that you treasure.

Write a Poem Like the speaker, most people feel torn between freedom and responsibility from time to time. Imagine that you are suddenly free of responsibilities. Write a poem describing where you would go and what you would do. Use personification to enhance your poem.

On With My Life

Patti Trull

I woke up with a start. For a moment, I couldn't remember where I was. Then I saw Linda sleeping in the other twin bed and remembered I was home and not in California. Oh, God! Today was Monday . . . the Day. The doctors had promised me I wouldn't have to stay at the hospital; they just wanted to talk to me. I'd heard that before and I didn't believe it now. I wanted to go back to sleep and wake up when it was all over. I didn't know what was wrong but I knew something was not right by the way people were behaving.

After breakfast Mom told Linda where all Teresa's things were. Annette, Cheryl, and Wayne were going to stay with friends for the day. I got dressed and then decided that I wasn't going to go. As long as I didn't go, Dr. Flashman couldn't tell me what they were going to do. I announced to my parents: "I'm not going today. The way I feel right now I may never go see Dr. Flashman again."

Patti Trull is told that she has cancer when she is fifteen years old—and that isn't the end of the bad news. How does Patti cope with her illness?

"Patti, you have to go."

"No I don't. You can't force me."

"Patti, we don't want to force you. We just want you to get well."

"I am well."

I ran to the bathroom and locked myself in. "I'm not going and that's it," I yelled. "I'd rather stay in here and starve to death than go back to that stupid hospital!"

They left me alone. A bathroom wasn't such a bad place to live. I had water and a toilet . . . What more did I need?

_____

I communicated best by screaming at whomever happened to be handy.

_____

My father was upset—not screaming upset—he just didn't know what to do next or how to get me to the doctor's office. My mom knew me. She had spent so much time with me the past months that she knew I was just blowing off steam and that once I got it out of my system I would go. She was right. Deep down I knew I had to go—I just wanted everyone to know that I hated the idea. I was not a complacent[1] child nor could I easily discuss my feelings about what was happening to me. I communicated best by screaming at whomever happened to be handy. I didn't do this with doctors or friends, only with my family. I knew that whatever I did or said they would still love me, even though I pushed it

[1] overly content

a few times. Thank God they lived through all the anger and resentment I had bottled up inside.

By one o'clock that afternoon I was tired of living in the bathroom and had made a deal with my parents. Dad and I would go to the hospital for the X-rays and then come home, pick up Mom, and go to Dr. Flashman's office to talk. I wouldn't have to stay at the hospital . . . just have the X-ray and leave. Dad was smoking one cigarette after another and I was biting my nails.

I went to the X-ray Department. During those past eight months I had gotten to know almost everyone in X-ray. I was feeling less upset now, and we were even laughing about something when a technician interrupted. "Patti, when you are through here they want you to go to the Hematology[2] Department."

[2] study of the blood

I thought, *But that wasn't part of the agreement.* Then they told me that my dad was waiting for me there, and I also felt better knowing that Hematology was *two* floors away from Admissions.

While my father waited for me, he had asked one of the doctors to give me a mild tranquilizer[3] to calm me down. Dad felt I would come totally unglued when we got to Dr. Flashman's office and got the news.

[3] a drug given to calm a person

Instead of giving me a tranquilizer, this doctor called me into his office.

"Who are you?" I asked.

"I'm the hematology fellow, Dr. Roberts. I started with the service the first of July. Dr. Chard is on vacation for the month."

Children's was a teaching hospital, and a lot of doctors rotated through there. I had been pretty patient about being seen by so many different doctors through the months but now I was getting tired of it. *What does this one want?* I thought. *Another review of my history?* He sat down on one side of the desk and asked me if I'd like to sit down. I didn't really want to but I did. *What was I doing in an office instead of an examining room? Where was my dad and who was this doctor?*

"Patricia, you know you have cancer," the doctor said.

I looked straight at him and said, "I do not. I have a tumor, but I do *not* have cancer." I was sure he had the wrong chart sitting in front of him.

"Patricia, you know you have cancer," the doctor said.

"Yes, you do, Patti. We didn't tell you earlier because your parents didn't want you to know until it was absolutely necessary. Now, that time has come."

What was he saying? Cancer! I could die from cancer!

"Am I going to die?"

"We don't know what is going to happen, Patti. We do know you can't continue to have that tumor in your leg grow and spread to other parts of your body. You are a very lucky person. Most people with this disease die within six months. For you it has been eight months, and things look very good. The problem with this disease is it can spread, or metastasize, to your lungs. If that happens, your chances of survival are very low."

"What is very low?"

"Less than five percent. Patti, remember you are lucky. Your tumor has not done that. We have every hope that you'll be okay. Patricia, because the tumor is in your upper thigh bone, we need to remove the entire bone. Unfortunately, the only way we can do this is to amputate your leg."

"DO WHAT?" I yelled. I looked down at my legs and could hardly see because of the tears. "How high would you have to amputate?"

"All the way to your hip—we have to make sure we get it all."

Where were Mom and Dad? And Dr. Chard? Did they know this? *Dear God! Please help me!* I got up and left the office. Still crying, I walked down and out the front door of the hospital. My mind couldn't absorb anything I had just heard. I sat on a bench, aware that children were laughing, people were coming and going. But it didn't matter. Nothing mattered. I felt as if the world had stopped and I had gotten off. I saw my father coming toward me.

"What's wrong?" he asked.

I just said, "You know what's wrong."

My father didn't know that I had been told or what had happened. He had been waiting for me to come back from X-ray. He asked me to sit there on the bench—he'd be back in a few minutes. When he came back about five minutes later, all he said was, "Let's go home."

I got into the car and felt like I was going to throw up. I cried and Dad talked. He said that he and my mother loved me very much and if one of them could take my place they would. They were proud of how I had handled the last eight months—they knew it hadn't been easy. He then told me that I didn't have to have the operation if I didn't want to. They would never force me into it. It would have to be my decision. I continued to cry.

"Dad . . . Thanks for not telling me any sooner."

We drove up the driveway and Mom was waiting on the front steps. I think it was the first time in her life she'd ever been on time. She wasn't giving me a chance to get out of the car and go through another scene. When she got into the backseat she asked me why I was crying. My father replied, "She knows."

Mom began to cry and then held on to me. "Patti, when this is all over we are going to Australia." Mom always dealt with stress by escaping.

By the time we reached downtown Seattle, the three of us had pulled our act together. I was ready to talk about what was going on. I had a lot of questions. When Dr. Flashman walked into the examining room I began to cry again. He told me that he was sorry and from that moment on he would always tell me the truth about what was going on with my disease.

He then looked at me and said, "Patti, how long do you think you've known?"

"I honestly had no idea this whole time that I have cancer. I figured there was something seriously wrong, but nobody ever let what it was slip. When I sat in the hematology waiting room and listened to mothers talking about their children having cancer, I'd think how lucky I was that my tumor wasn't malignant.[4] I can't believe that I was so blind! I had no idea until today." I cried some more.

[4] likely to cause death

The phone rang, and Dr. Flashman became even more serious. "Patricia. Mr. and Mrs. Trull. I'm afraid that I have some more bad news. That was Children's. The X-ray taken this morning showed a tumor in the lower lobe of Patti's right lung. The radiologist[5] could only see one, but they want her right back this afternoon for more X-rays, called tomograms."

[5] one who takes X-rays of bones or organs in the body

I couldn't believe what I was hearing. Not only did I have cancer and need my leg amputated, now I had a tumor in my lung and my chances of survival just blew out the window. I remembered the saying, "God never gives you more than you can bear." Well, He sure pushed me to the limit that day. I was in shock and felt as if I would never move again. Dr. Flashman talked to my parents, but I don't remember anything he said. I just kept thinking, *What am I going to do? What is going to happen next?* At that point I don't think that I felt anything. I couldn't cry . . . or talk . . . or even think about the future. The whole situation was just too much.

We went back to the hospital for the tomograms and then went home. I was exhausted and just wanted to go to bed. Linda met us at the door with Teresa in her arms.

"Hey, I thought you were going to the hospital for an operation," she said.

"I've been there, Linda. I've got leg cancer, lung cancer, I need my leg amputated, and I'm probably going to die. I'm going to bed."

Sleep had always been a good escape for me. I have never lost a night's sleep from worry—from pain, maybe—but not worry. I woke up long enough for dinner, then went back to bed. Friends had been calling and wanted to know how I was. They thought I was in the hospital. All they were told was that I was home and not in the hospital and would talk to them the next day. I didn't want to talk to anyone; I just wanted to sleep.

I've got leg cancer, lung cancer, I need my leg amputated, and I'm probably going to die. I'm going to bed.

---

[6] treatment of disease with special drugs

[7] injuries or changes in an organ or tissue of the body

Later that night I woke up and again began to wonder what was next. The doctors were having another tumor conference to decide if they should go ahead with surgery, try more chemotherapy,[6] or leave me alone. It all depended on how many lesions[7] were in my lungs.

I got up and played with Teresa for a while. She was two months old and a good distraction for me. I enjoyed feeding and rocking her. Mom came in and told me that the hospital had called earlier. They had decided to give me ten weeks of a new type of chemotherapy drug. I would only have to take it every other week (five doses). I was lucky because the X-ray had shown only one lesion. They wouldn't do any surgery on my leg until they knew if they could control the tumor in my lung.

I was ecstatic! *Time!* I had just bought ten weeks—two-and-a-half months of *time* before they would even consider amputating my leg. For a fifteen-year-old, losing a leg is a very real thing—dying is not. What a deal. A shot only every other week. I hadn't had a shot-free week in ages.

We tried to make the most of those ten weeks. We had a month before school started, so we rented a beach house and packed everyone and everything up for a few weeks' vacation. Linda stayed a while, but then went home after reassuring me everything was going to be just fine. She was mostly trying to reassure herself. The new medicine didn't bother me and I had no side effects. The worst part was just trying to get it into my veins. I didn't tell everyone at school about the possibility of losing my leg, only a few close girl friends. The rest eventually heard it through the grapevine.

I was only seven weeks away from my sixteenth birthday, so I was busy practicing my driving. No matter what, I was going to get my license.

Most of the time during those weeks, I just enjoyed life and tried to forget. I was a great denier, and that was how I coped. I couldn't dwell on the bad things because I knew the problems weren't going to go away. I also knew that thinking about them didn't help me. When something tragic happens or someone dies you feel like everyone should stop and feel your sadness too. But life goes on and you either go with it or you stop living—and I didn't want to stop living.

About the Author

Patti Trull was born in 1952 in Seattle, Washington. She wrote the book *On With My Life* to tell about her struggle with cancer. Patti learned to accept the fact that she would lose her leg and faced the operation with courage and determination. After her surgery, she got her driver's license and continued to lead an active, productive life. Patti graduated from high school with her class and went on to college, where she earned a degree in occupational therapy. She later worked with young cancer patients and their families.

Responding to the Autobiography

▼ Think Back

What emotions does Patti exhibit on the morning of the hospital visit? Why?

How does Patti react to the news that she has cancer?

How does Patti come to accept her illness?

▼ Discuss

Why didn't Patti's parents and doctors tell her sooner that she had cancer? Do you think they should have told her sooner? Why or why not?

Time is a precious commodity when one is faced with a life-threatening illness like cancer. Patti did whatever she could to enjoy life. What would you have done? What other ways are there to cope with serious illnesses or situations that are traumatic?

▼ Write

Write Dialogue By using authentic dialogue, Patti Trull shows the reader how the events actually happened. Skim the selection, paying particular attention to the dialogue. Rewrite several scenes that contain dialogue, using words and phrases that you might use.

Write a Personal Narrative Think about a traumatic or joyous time in your life. Can you recall the conversations that took place then? Write a personal narrative that describes that time in your life. Use dialogue to make your account more interesting and realistic.

The White Umbrella

G i s h   J e n

hen I was twelve, my mother went to work without telling me or my little sister.

"Not that we need the second income." The lilt of her accent drifted from the kitchen up to the top of the stairs, where Mona and I were listening.

"No," said my father, in a barely audible[1] voice. "Not like the Lee family."

The Lees were the only other Chinese family in town. I remembered how sorry my parents had felt for Mrs. Lee when she started waitressing downtown the year before; and so when my mother began coming home late, I didn't say anything, and tried to keep Mona from saying anything either.

"But why shouldn't I?" she argued. "Lots of people's mothers work."

"Those are American people," I said.

"So what do you think we are? I can do the Pledge of Allegiance with my eyes closed."

A young Chinese-American girl is embarrassed when her mother takes a job. How does a white umbrella fit into the picture?

[1] able to be heard

Nevertheless, she tried to be discreet;[2] and if my mother wasn't home by 5:30, we would start cooking by ourselves, to make sure dinner would be on time. Mona would wash the vegetables and put on the rice; I would chop.

For weeks we wondered what kind of work she was doing. I imagined that she was selling perfume, testing dessert recipes for the local newspaper. Or maybe she was working for the florist. Now that she had learned to drive, she might be delivering boxes of roses to people.

"I don't think so," said Mona as we walked to our piano lesson after school. "She would've hit something by now."

A gust of wind littered the street with leaves.

"Maybe we better hurry up," she went on, looking at the sky. "It's going to pour."

"But we're too early." Her lesson didn't begin until 4:00, mine until 4:30, so we usually tried to walk as slowly as we could. "And anyway, those aren't the kind of clouds that rain. Those are cumulus clouds."

We arrived out of breath and wet.

"Oh, you poor, poor dears," said old Miss Crosman. "Why don't you call me the next time it's like this out? If your mother won't drive you, I can come pick you up."

"No, that's okay," I answered. Mona wrung her hair out on Miss Crosman's rug. "We just couldn't get the roof of our car to close, is all. We took it to the beach last summer and got sand in the mechanism." I pronounced this last word carefully, as if the credibility[3] of my lie

[2] careful and sensible

[3] believability

depended on its middle syllable. "It's never been the same." I thought for a second. "It's a convertible."

"Well then make yourselves at home." She exchanged looks with Eugenie Roberts, whose lesson we were interrupting. Eugenie smiled good-naturedly. "The towels are in the closet across from the bathroom."

Huddling at the end of Miss Crosman's nine-foot leatherette couch, Mona and I watched Eugenie play. She was a grade ahead of me and, according to school rumor, had a boyfriend in high school. I believed it. Aside from her ballooning breasts—which threatened to collide with the keyboard as she played—she had auburn hair, blue eyes, and, I noted with a particular pang, a pure white, folding umbrella.

"I can't see," whispered Mona.

"So clean your glasses."

"My glasses *are* clean. You're in the way."

I looked at her. "They look dirty to me."

"That's because *your* glasses are dirty."

Eugenie came bouncing to the end of her piece.

"Oh! Just stupendous!"[4] Miss Crosman hugged her, then looked up as Eugenie's mother walked in. "Stupendous!" she said again. "Oh! Mrs. Roberts! Your daughter has a gift, a real gift. It's an honor to teach her."

Mrs. Roberts, radiant with pride, swept her daughter out of the room as if she were royalty, born to the piano bench. Watching the way Eugenie carried herself, I sat up, and concentrated so hard on sucking in my stomach that I did not realize until the Robertses were gone that Eugenie had left her umbrella. As Mona

[4] outstanding, marvelous

began to play, I jumped up and ran to the window, meaning to call to them—only to see their brake lights flash then fade at the stop sign at the corner. As if to allow them passage, the rain had let up; a quivering sun lit their way.

The umbrella glowed like a scepter[5] on the blue carpet while Mona, slumping over the keyboard, managed to eke out a fair rendition[6] of a catfight. At the end of the piece, Miss Crosman asked her to stand up.

"Stay right there," she said, then came back a minute later with a towel to cover the bench. "You must be cold," she continued. "Shall I call your mother and have her bring over some dry clothes?"

"No," answered Mona. "She won't come because she . . ."

"She's too busy," I broke in from the back of the room.

"I see." Miss Crosman sighed and shook her head a little. "Your glasses are filthy, honey," she said to Mona. "Shall I clean them for you?"

Sisterly embarrassment seized me. Why hadn't Mona wiped her lenses when I told her to? As she resumed abuse of the piano, I stared at the umbrella. I wanted to open it, twirl it around by its slender silver handle; I wanted to dangle it from my wrist on the way to school the way the other girls did. I wondered what Miss Crosman would say if I offered to bring it to Eugenie at school tomorrow. She would be impressed with my consideration for others; Eugenie would be pleased to have it back; and I would have possession of

[5] staff carried by a ruler as a symbol of power

[6] performance

the umbrella for an entire night. I looked at it again, toying with the idea of asking for one for Christmas. I knew, however, how my mother would react.

"Things," she would say. "What's the matter with a raincoat? All you want is things, just like an American."

Sitting down for my lesson, I was careful to keep the towel under me and sit up straight.

"I'll bet you can't see a thing either," said Miss Crosman, reaching for my glasses. "And you can relax, you poor dear." She touched my chest, in an area where she never would have touched Eugenie Roberts. "This isn't a boot camp."

When Miss Crosman finally allowed me to start playing I played extra well, as well as I possibly could. See, I told her with my fingers. You don't have to feel sorry for me.

"That was wonderful," said Miss Crosman. "Oh! Just wonderful."

An entire constellation[7] rose in my heart.

"And guess what," I announced proudly. "I have a surprise for you."

Then I played a second piece for her, a much more difficult one that she had not assigned.

"Oh! That was stupendous," she said without hugging me. "Stupendous! You are a genius, young lady. If your mother had started you younger, you'd be playing like Eugenie Roberts by now!"

I looked at the keyboard, wishing that I had still a third, even more difficult piece to play for her.

[7] brightness, like that of stars

I wanted to tell her that I was the school spelling bee champion, that I wasn't ticklish, that I could do karate.

"My mother is a concert pianist," I said.

She looked at me for a long moment, then finally, without saying anything, hugged me. I didn't say anything about bringing the umbrella to Eugenie at school.

The steps were dry when Mona and I sat down to wait for my mother.

"Do you want to wait inside?" Miss Crosman looked anxiously at the sky.

"No," I said. "Our mother will be here any minute."

"In a while," said Mona.

"Any minute," I said again, even though my mother had been at least twenty minutes late every week since she started working.

According to the church clock across the street we had been waiting twenty-five minutes when Miss Crosman came out again.

"Shall I give you ladies a ride home?"

"No," I said. "Our mother is coming any minute."

"Shall I at least give her a call to remind her you're here? Maybe she forgot about you."

"I don't think she forgot," said Mona.

"Shall I give her a call anyway? Just to be safe?"

"I bet she already left," I said. "How could she forget about us?"

Miss Crosman went in to call.

"There's no answer," she said, coming back out.

"See, she's on her way," I said.

"Are you sure you wouldn't like to come in?"

"No," said Mona.

"Yes," I said. I pointed at my sister. "She meant yes, too. She meant no, she wouldn't like to go in."

Miss Crosman looked at her watch. "It's 5:30 now, ladies. My pot roast will be coming out in fifteen minutes. Maybe you'd like to come in and have some then?"

"My mother's almost here," I said. "She's on her way."

We watched and watched the street. I tried to imagine what my mother was doing; I tried to imagine her writing messages in the sky, even though I knew she was afraid of planes. I watched as the branches of Miss Crosman's big willow tree started to sway; they had all been trimmed to exactly the same height off the ground, so that they looked beautiful, like hair in the wind.

It started to rain.

"Miss Crosman is coming out again," said Mona.

"Don't let her talk you into going inside," I whispered.

"Why not?"

"Because that would mean Mom isn't really coming any minute."

"But she isn't," said Mona. "She's *working*."

"Shhh! Miss Crosman is going to hear you."

"She's working! She's working! She's working!"

I put my hand over her mouth, but she licked it, and so I was wiping my hand on my wet dress when the front door opened.

"We're getting even *wetter*," said Mona right away. "Wetter and wetter."

"Shall we all go in?" Miss Crosman pulled Mona to her feet. "Before you young ladies catch pneumonia? You've been out here an hour already."

"We're *freezing*." Mona looked up at Miss Crosman. "Do you have any hot chocolate? We're going to catch *pneumonia*."

"I'm not going in," I said. "My mother's coming any minute.

"Come on," said Mona. "Use your *noggin*."

"Any minute."

"Come on, Mona," Miss Crosman opened the door. "Shall we get you inside first?"

"See you in the hospital," said Mona as she went in. "See you in the hospital with *pneumonia*."

I stared out into the empty street. The rain was pricking me all over; I was cold; I wanted to go inside. I wanted to be able to let myself go inside. If Miss Crosman came out again, I decided, I would go in.

She came out with a blanket and the white umbrella.

I could not believe that I was actually holding the umbrella, opening it. It sprang up by itself as if it were alive, as if that were what it wanted to do—as if it belonged in my hands, above my head. I stared up at the network of silver spokes, then spun the umbrella around and around and around. It was so clean and white that it seemed to glow, to illuminate everything around it.

"It's beautiful," I said.

Miss Crosman sat down next to me, on one end of the blanket. I moved the umbrella over so that it covered that too. I could feel the rain on my left shoulder and shivered. She put her arm around me.

"You poor, poor dear."

I knew that I was in store for another bolt of sympathy, and braced myself by staring up into the umbrella.

"You know, I very much wanted to have children when I was younger," she continued.

"You did?"

She stared at me a minute. Her face looked dry and crusty, like day-old frosting.

"I did. But then I never got married."

I twirled the umbrella around again.

"This is the most beautiful umbrella I have ever seen," I said. "Ever, in my whole life."

"Do you have an umbrella?"

"No. But my mother's going to get me one just like this for Christmas."

"Is she? I tell you what. You don't have to wait until Christmas. You can have this one."

"But this one belongs to Eugenie Roberts," I protested. "I have to give it back to her tomorrow in school."

"Who told you it belongs to Eugenie? It's not Eugenie's. It's mine. And now I'm giving it to you, so it's yours."

"It is?"

She hugged me tighter. "That's right. It's all yours."

"It's mine?" I didn't know what to say. "Mine?" Suddenly I was jumping up and down in the rain. "It's beautiful! Oh! It's beautiful!" I laughed.

Miss Crosman laughed, too, even though she was getting all wet.

"Thank you, Miss Crosman. Thank you very much. Thanks a zillion. It's beautiful. It's *stupendous!*"

"You're quite welcome," she said.

"Thank you," I said again, but that didn't seem like enough. Suddenly I knew just what she wanted to hear. "I wish you were my mother."

Right away I felt bad.

"You shouldn't say that," she said, but her face was opening into a huge smile as the lights of my mother's car cautiously turned the corner. I quickly collapsed the umbrella and put it up my skirt, holding onto it from the outside, through the material.

"Mona!" I shouted into the house. "Mona! Hurry up! Mom's here! I told you she was coming."

Then I ran away from Miss Crosman, down the curb. Mona came tearing up to my side as my mother neared the house. We both backed up a few feet, so that in case she went onto the curb, she wouldn't run us over.

"But why didn't you go inside with Mona!" my mother asked on the way home. She had taken off her own coat to put over me, and had the heat on high.

"She wasn't using her noggin," said Mona, next to me in the back seat.

"I should call next time," said my mother. "I just don't like to say where I am."

That was when she finally told us that she was working as a check-out clerk in the A&P. She was supposed to be on the day shift, but the other employees were unreliable, and her boss had promised her a promotion if she would stay until the evening shift filled in.

For a moment no one said anything. Even Mona seemed to find the revelation[8] disappointing.

"A promotion already!" she said, finally.

I listened to the windshield wipers.

"You're so quiet." My mother looked at me in the rearview mirror. "What's the matter?"

"I wish you would quit," I said after a moment.

She sighed. "The Chinese have a saying: one beam cannot hold the roof up."

"But Eugenie Roberts's father supports their family."

She sighed once more. "Eugenie Roberts's father is Eugenie Roberts's father," she said.

As we entered the downtown area, Mona started leaning hard against me every time the car turned right, trying to push me over. Remembering what I had said to Miss Crosman, I tried to maneuver the umbrella under my leg so she wouldn't feel it.

"What's under your skirt?" Mona wanted to know as we came to a traffic light. My mother, watching us in the rearview mirror again, rolled slowly to a stop.

"What's the matter?" she asked.

"There's something under her skirt." said Mona, pulling at me.

"Under her skirt?"

Meanwhile, a man crossing the street started to yell at us. "Who do you think you are, lady?" he said. "You're blocking the whole damn crosswalk."

We all froze. Other people walking by stopped to watch.

"Didn't you hear me?" he went on, starting to thump on the hood with his fist. "Don't you speak English?"

My mother began to back up, but the car behind us honked. Luckily, the light turned green right after that. She sighed in relief.

"What were you saying, Mona?" she asked.

We wouldn't have hit the car behind us that hard if he hadn't been moving, too, but as it was our car bucked violently, throwing us all first back and then forward.

"Uh oh," said Mona when we stopped. "*Another* accident."

I was relieved to have attention diverted[9] from the umbrella. Then I noticed my mother's head, tilted back onto the seat. Her eyes were closed.

"Mom!" I screamed. "Mom! Wake up!"

She opened her eyes. "Please don't yell," she said. "Enough people are going to yell already."

"I thought you were dead," I said, starting to cry. "I thought you were dead."

She turned around, looked at me intently, then put her hand on my forehead.

"Sick," she confirmed. "Some kind of sick is giving you crazy ideas."

[9] turned away

As the man from the car behind us started tapping on the window, I moved the umbrella away from my leg. Then Mona and my mother were getting out of the car. I got out after them; and while everyone else was inspecting the damage we'd done, I threw the umbrella down a sewer.

About the Author

Gish Jen's real first name is Lillian. High school friends nicknamed her "Gish" after Lillian Gish, an actress who had a long career on the stage and in movies. Jen has taught writing classes at Tufts University and the University of Massachusetts. Her fiction has appeared in many magazines and anthologies, including *Best American Short Stories of 1988*. Jen's novels include *Typical American* and *Mona in the Promised Land*.

Responding to the Story

▼ Think Back

Why did the narrator place so much value on the white umbrella?

Why does the narrator admire Eugenie Roberts?

Why are the sisters afraid to tell anyone that their mother is working?

▼ Discuss

Why do you think the narrator would say that she wished Miss Crosman was her mother?

Even though she thought the umbrella was beautiful, the narrator soon discards it. Why?

What does the narrator learn about herself and her mother?

▼ Write

Write a Description Gish Jen makes her characters seem real by using dialogue and detailed descriptions of their appearance and actions. Write a short descriptive paragraph about a sibling, parent, or teacher. Use dialogue and detailed descriptions to make the person seem real.

Write an Essay Because they were Chinese-Americans, the narrator's family often felt like outsiders. In a brief essay, describe an incident or period in your life when you felt like you were an outsider. Use the techniques of characterization to describe yourself and others.

Freedom

C h a r l o t t e   P a i n t e r

*When her husband died, Alice Lindberg Snyder was deeply
shaken. To cope with her loss, Snyder went through
counseling. This experience helped her discover talents and
needs she didn't know she had. Though in her seventies, she
learned to live each day to the fullest.*

**How old is too old?
When a 70-year-old
woman follows her
dream, what will other
people think of her?**

The tap shoes she wanted were in the window
of the Children's Bootery, so she went inside
and asked for them. The salesman raised his
eyebrows but lifted her foot onto his metal measure,
out of habit maybe. She told him her size, said it
hadn't changed in sixty years. Nice that they measure
the children's feet every time, she thought, but this was
her second childhood, not her first. "You been dancing
that long too?" the young man asked.

"Just started," she said. Had a talent for it too, but
she didn't boast. Actually she did dance as a child and
had had a few more lessons lately. The shoes were a
must now, especially since Edie's call.

"You'd better come on and visit now, Alice. You're going to get old. You're going to die like everybody else, so *do it now*!" By most standards she was ancient already, so *now* was the time.

All those things she hadn't done when Bill was alive she had begun to do now just because they were in her, the perfectly harmless things she had done as a young girl: sailing, swimming, whistling, tap-dancing. That fun-loving nature of her childhood hadn't died; she just hadn't turned it loose all those years. Now it was taking over. Let other people worry about brittle bones if they wanted to—that was their lookout. Or the impropriety[1] of an old woman who sticks her fingers between her teeth to hail a cab. Let them think her a zany eccentric[2] if they liked. She was through with neglecting the part of herself that wanted to play.

[1] improper behavior

[2] a person who behaves oddly

She was thinking of taking her grandson rafting on the Rogue River with a friend of his. Better not wait on that. And of going with Edie to the Hebrides to hear the wind shriek in their ears.

"Do you think it's unusual for someone my age to tap?" she asked the shoe salesman.

"Unusual but okay by me," the salesman grinned and tied the bow on the tap shoes for her. "How about a demonstration?"

"Move that stool aside," she said. "I'll show you something right here." Still sitting in her chair, she let her feet beat a quick rhythm on the vinyl floor and hummed "The Sidewalks of New York." The salesman was impressed. "You see, it'd be great therapy for somebody in a wheelchair. Anyone can learn to tap-dance."

The salesman wrapped up the shoes. "And I'll have one of those balloons you give away too, please," she said.

Alice was into taboo-busting. She wasn't going to sit back and be the widow of a university professor who limited herself to activity suitable to her years and status. She had poured at her last faculty tea. Now she was going to become all that she could be.

About the Author

Charlotte Painter taught at Stanford University and the University of California at Berkeley and at Santa Cruz. She is the coauthor, with Mary Jane Moffett, of *Revelations: Diaries of Women*. Painter's stories and poems have been published in many magazines.

Responding to the Essay

▼ Think Back

How did the shoe salesman react to Alice's purchasing tap shoes?

What event convinced Alice to take up dancing? Why?

How does Alice feel about her life? What details give you clues about her feelings?

▼ Discuss

What did Alice want to do before it was too late? Why was this a turning point in Alice's life? What adventures do you want to have in your lifetime?

Alice Lindberg Snyder enjoyed breaking taboos—things thought by society to be improper or unacceptable. What are some taboos with which you are familiar? Do you think they should be broken?

▼ Write

Convey the Tone Throughout the selection, Charlotte Painter writes as if she herself were seventy years old, with no time to waste. Her matter-of-fact tone is very supportive of Alice. She agrees with Alice's actions and wants the reader to view her as she does. Try rewriting a passage from "Freedom" with a different tone.

Write an Essay Write a short essay describing your thoughts about a specific taboo. As you write, think about the tone of your essay.

Theme Links

Turning Points

In this unit, you've read about people who faced turning points that sent them down new paths in life. You have also thought about incidents or experiences that changed your life and perhaps led you to look at the world in a new light.

▼ Group Discussion

With a partner or in a small group, talk about the selections in this unit and how they relate to the theme and to your own lives. Use questions like the following to guide the discussion.

• What turning points do the people and characters in this unit experience? What is significant about them?
• Which turning point can you relate to?
• Of the people you read about in this unit, which ones experienced a turning point without realizing it? Do you think this happens to many people? Explain.

▼ The Characters: Monologue

Imagine you are a person or character from one of the selections in this unit. What would that person say about the turning point she or he experiences? Write a short monologue to recite to your class about how your life has changed and what it will be like in the future.

▼ The Characters: Patti and Alice

What do Patti Trull and Alice Lindberg Snyder have in common? Role-play a conversation between the girl and the woman discussing their plans for the next year.

▼ Your Choice

Often a decision must be made at a turning point in life. Choose a selection from this unit in which a character made a choice. Then imagine that he or she made a different choice. How would the selection be different? Write a new ending for the selection reflecting that different choice.

▼ The Theme and You

What has been the most important turning point in your life? Write a "Before and After" essay describing how your life changed. Your essay should include answers to the following questions.

- What happened?
- Did the incident change me? How?
- What were things like before this turning point?
- How were things different after this?

Before you begin writing, you might want to make a chart like the one below to help you choose your topic.

Turning Point	Before	After
We moved from Iowa to New York City.	I lived on a farm. I had really good friends.	I lived in an apartment building. I felt like an outsider.
My little brother got leukemia.	I teased my brother a lot. I was jealous. I wanted my own way.	I learned I loved my brother. I helped my parents take care of him.

Families

Who are the members of your family? How well do you know them all? How is your relationship different with different people in your family?

Families are not all alike. Each family has its own unique personal, cultural, and religious beliefs and customs. For most of us, our families are the center of our lives and our first classroom. We learn about life, love, responsibilities—and especially about ourselves—through our relationships with family members.

The selections in this unit describe a
variety of family relationships. As you
read, think about your relationships with
the members of your family. What are they
like now? What might they be like in the
future?

A New Arrival

Shirley Jackson

Shirley Jackson tells what her young children think of their new brother. Is their reaction what she expects?

I t was a beautiful morning, cold and clear and full of color, and the taxi driver was just finishing a story about how his wife's mother had come to visit them and canned all the peaches his wife had been planning to put into their freezer. "Just wasted the whole lot of them," he said, and pulled up in front of the house with a flourish.

"There are the children on the porch," I said.

"Beginning to seem like Christmas," my husband said to the taxi driver as I got out, and the taxi driver said, "Snow before morning."

Jannie's hair had obviously not been combed since I left, and as I went up the front walk I was resolving to make her tell immediately where she had hidden the hairbrush. She was wearing her dearest summer sundress, and she was barefoot. Laurie needed a haircut, and he had on his old sneakers, one of which no longer laces, but fastens with a safety pin; I had made a particular point of throwing those sneakers into the garbage can before I left. Sally had chocolate all over her face and *she* was wearing Laurie's fur hat. All three of them were leaning over the porch rail, still and expectant.[1]

[1] anticipating something

I tried to catch hold of all three of them at once, but they evaded[2] me skillfully and ran at their father. "Did you bring it?" Jannie demanded, "did you bring it, did you bring it, did you bring it?"

[2] avoided; got away from

"Is *that* it you're carrying?" Laurie demanded sternly, "that *little* thing?"

"Did you *bring* it?" Jannie insisted.

"Come indoors and I'll show you," their father said.

They followed him into the living room, and stood in a solemn row by the couch. "Now don't touch," their father said, and they nodded all together. They watched while he carefully set the bundle down on the couch and unwrapped it.

Then, into the stunned silence which followed, Sally finally said, "What is it?"

"It's a baby," said their father, with an edge of nervousness to his voice, "it's a baby boy and its name is Barry."

"What's a baby?" Sally asked me.

"It's pretty small," Laurie said doubtfully. "Is that the best you could get?"

"I tried to get another, a bigger one," I said with irritation, "but the doctor said this was the only one left."

"My goodness," said Jannie, "what are we going to do with *that*? Anyway," she said, "*you're* back."

Suddenly she and Sally were both climbing onto my lap at once, and Laurie came closer and allowed me to kiss him swiftly on the cheek; I discovered that I could reach around all three of them, something I had not been able to do for some time.

"Well," Laurie said, anxious to terminate[3] this sentimental scene, "so now we've got this baby. Do you think it will grow?" he asked his father.

"It's got very small feet," Jannie said. "I really believe they're *too* small."

"Well, if you don't like it we can *always* take it back," said their father.

"Oh, we like it all right, I guess," Laurie said comfortingly. "It's only that I guess we figured on something a little bigger."

"What *is* it?" asked Sally, unconvinced. She put out a tentative[4] finger and touched one toe. "Is this its foot?"

"Please start calling it 'him'," I said.

"Him?" said Sally. "Him?"

"Hi, Barry," said Laurie, leaning down to look directly into one open blue eye, "hi, Barry, hi, Barry, hi, Barry."

"Hi, Barry," said Jannie.

"Hi, Barry," said Sally. "Is this your foot?"

"I suppose it'll cry a lot?" Laurie asked his father, man to man.

His father shrugged. "Not much else it *can* do," he pointed out.

"I remember Jannie cried all the time," Laurie went on.

[3] end

[4] timid; hesitant

"I did not," Jannie said. "*You* were the one cried all the time."

"Did you get it at the hospital?" Sally asked. She moved Barry's foot up and down and he curled his toes.

"Yes," I said.

"Why didn't you take me?" Sally asked.

"I took you the last time," I said.

"What did you say its name was?" Sally asked.

"Barry," I said.

"Barry?"

"Barry."

"Where did you get it?"

"Well," Laurie said. He sighed and stretched. "Better take a look at those Greek tetradrachms,"[5] he said.

[5] ancient Greek silver coins

"Right," said his father, rising.

"Jannie, you go find that hairbrush," I said.

Laurie, on his way out of the room, stopped next to me and hesitated, obviously trying to think of something congratulatory to say. "I guess it *will* be nice for you, though," he said at last. "Something to keep you busy now *we're* all grown up."

About the Author

Shirley Jackson (1919–1965) was born in San Francisco, California, and moved to New York as a teenager. She and her husband later moved to Vermont. "A New Arrival" was taken from *Life Among the Savages*, a collection of stories about their family.

Responding to the Story

▼ Think Back

Where are Shirley Jackson and her husband returning from at the beginning of "A New Arrival"? What are they bringing home?

How does each of Shirley Jackson's children react to the new baby?

Why does Laurie agree at the end that the baby will be a good addition to the family?

▼ Discuss

Jackson does not explain what *it* is immediately. Why do you think she does this?

Jackson and her husband play along with their children's confusion about babies. How would you have handled the situation? Why?

▼ Write

Write a Funny Story How does Jackson humorously describe each of her children when she sees them standing on the porch? Write a humorous story about something you believed as a child, such as what causes thunder or how the man got into the moon.

Write a Journal Entry Imagine that you are a young child meeting a new baby brother or sister for the first time. Write a journal entry telling how you feel. What would you say to your parents about the baby? Are some of your comments funny? Why?

Así es la Vida

An Hour with Abuelo

Judith Ortiz Cofer

J ust one hour, *una hora*, is all I'm asking of you, son." My grandfather is in a nursing home in Brooklyn, and my mother wants me to spend some time with him, since the doctors say that he doesn't have too long to go now. I don't have much time left of my summer vacation, and there's a stack of books next to my bed I've got to read if I'm going to get into the AP English class I want. I'm going stupid in some of my classes, and Mr. Williams, the principal at Central, said that if I passed some reading tests, he'd let me move up.

Besides, I hate the place, the old people's home, especially the way it smells like industrial-strength ammonia and other stuff I won't mention, since it turns my stomach. And really the *abuelo* always has a lot of relatives visiting him, so I've gotten out of going out there except at Christmas, when a whole vanload of grandchildren are herded over there to give him gifts and a hug. We all make it quick and spend the rest of

Visiting a nursing home isn't this teenager's idea of a good time. What does his grandfather do that takes Arturo by surprise?

the time in the recreation area, where they play checkers and stuff with some of the old people's games, and I catch up on back issues of *Modern Maturity*. I'm not picky, I'll read almost anything.

Anyway, after my mother nags me for about a week, I let her drive me to Golden Years. She drops me off in front. She wants me to go in alone and have a "good time" talking to Abuelo. I tell her to be back in one hour or I'll take the bus back to Paterson. She squeezes my hand and says, "*Gracias, hijo,*" in a choked-up voice like I'm doing her a big favor.

I get depressed the minute I walk into the place. They line up the old people in wheelchairs in the hallway as if they were about to be raced to the finish line by orderlies who don't even look at them when they push them here and there. I walk fast to room 10, Abuelo's "suite." He is sitting up in his bed writing with a pencil in one of those old-fashioned black hardback notebooks. It has the outline of the island of Puerto Rico on it. I slide into the hard vinyl chair by his bed. He sort of smiles and the lines on his face get deeper, but he doesn't say anything. Since I'm supposed to talk to him, I say, "What are you doing, Abuelo, writing the story of your life?"

It's supposed to be a joke, but he answers, "*Sí*, how did you know, Arturo?"

His name is Arturo too. I was named after him. I don't really know my grandfather. His children, including my mother, came to New York and New Jersey (where I was born) and he stayed on the Island until my grandmother died. Then he got sick, and since nobody could leave their jobs to go take care of him, they brought him to this nursing home in Brooklyn. I see him a couple of times a year, but he's always surrounded by his sons and daughters. My mother tells me that Don Arturo had once been a teacher back in Puerto Rico, but had lost his job after the war. Then he became a farmer. She's always saying in a sad voice, "*Ay, bendito!* What a waste of a fine mind." Then she usually shrugs her shoulders and says, "*Así es la vida.*" That's the way life is. It sometimes makes me mad that the adults I know just accept whatever is thrown at them because "that's the way things are." Not for me. I go after what I want.

Anyway, Abuelo is looking at me like he was trying to see into my head, but he doesn't say anything. Since I like stories, I decide I may as well ask him if he'll read me what he wrote.

I look at my watch: I've already used up twenty minutes of the hour I promised my mother.

Abuelo starts talking in his slow way. He speaks what my mother calls book English. He taught himself from a dictionary, and his words sound stiff, like he's sounding them out in his head before he says them. With his children he speaks Spanish, and that funny book English with us grandchildren. I'm surprised that he's still so sharp, because his body is shrinking like a crumpled-up brown paper sack with some bones in it. But I can see from looking into his eyes that the light is still on in there.

"It is a short story, Arturo. The story of my life. It will not take very much time to read it."

"I have time, Abuelo." I'm a little embarrassed that he saw me looking at my watch.

"Yes, *hijo*. You have spoken the truth. *La verdad*. You have much time."

Abuelo reads: "'I loved words from the beginning of my life. In the *campo*[1] where I was born one of seven sons, there were few books. My mother read them to us over and over: the Bible, the stories of Spanish conquistadors[2] and of pirates that she had read as a child and brought with her from the city of Mayagüez; that was before she married my father, a coffee bean farmer; and she taught us words from the newspaper that a boy on a horse brought every week to her. She taught each of us how to write on a slate with chalks that she ordered by mail every year. We used those chalks until they were so small that you lost them between your fingers.

"'I always wanted to be a writer and a teacher. With my heart and my soul I knew that I wanted to be around books all of my life. And so against the wishes of my father, who wanted all his sons to help him on the land, she sent me to high school in Mayagüez. For four years I boarded with a couple she knew. I paid my rent in labor, and I ate vegetables I grew myself. I wore my clothes until they were thin as parchment. But I graduated at the top of my class! My whole family came to see me that day. My mother brought me a beautiful *guayabera*, a white shirt made of the finest cotton and embroidered by her own hands. I was a happy young man.

[1] *Spanish:* camp

[2] Spanish explorers who fought and conquered Mexico and other countries in the sixteenth century

"In those days you could teach in a country school with a high school diploma. So I went back to my mountain village and got a job teaching all grades in a little classroom built by the parents of my students.

"I had books sent to me by the government. I felt like a rich man although the pay was very small. I had books. All the books I wanted! I taught my students how to read poetry and plays, and how to write them. We made up songs and put on shows for the parents. It was a beautiful time for me.

"Then the war came, and the American President said that all Puerto Rican men would be drafted. I wrote to our governor and explained that I was the only teacher in the mountain village. I told him that the children would go back to the fields and grow up ignorant if I could not teach them their letters. I said that I thought I was a better teacher than a soldier. The governor did not answer my letter. I went into the U.S. Army.

"I told my sergeant that I could be a teacher in the army. I could teach all the farm boys their letters so that they could read the instructions on the ammunition boxes and not blow themselves up. The sergeant said I was too smart for my own good, and gave me a job cleaning latrines. He said to me there is reading material for you there, scholar. Read the writing on the walls. I spent the war mopping floors and cleaning toilets.

"When I came back to the Island, things had changed. You had to have a college degree to teach school, even the lower grades. My parents were sick, two of my brothers had been killed in the war, the others had stayed in Nueva York. I was the only one left to help the old people. I became a farmer. I married a good woman who gave me many good children. I taught them all how to read and write before they started school.'"

Abuelo then puts the notebook down on his lap and closes his eyes.

"*Así es la vida* is the title of my book," he says in a whisper, almost to himself. Maybe he's forgotten that I'm there.

For a long time he doesn't say anything else. I think that he's sleeping, but then I see that he's watching me through half-closed lids, maybe waiting for my opinion of his writing. I'm trying to think of something nice to say. I liked it and all, but not the title. And I think that he could've been a teacher if he had wanted to bad enough. Nobody is going to stop me from doing what I want with my life. I'm not going to let *la vida* get in my way. I want to discuss this with him, but the words are not coming into my head in Spanish just yet. I'm about to ask him why he didn't keep fighting to make his dream come true, when an old lady in hot-pink running shoes sort of appears at the door.

She is wearing a pink jogging outfit too. The world's oldest marathoner, I say to myself. She calls out to my grandfather in a flirty voice, "Yoo-hoo, Arturo, remember what day this is? It's poetry-reading day in the rec room! You promised us you'd read your new one today."

I see my abuelo perking up almost immediately. He points to his wheelchair, which is hanging like a huge metal bat in the open closet. He makes it obvious that he wants me to get it. I put it together, and with Mrs. Pink Running Shoes's help, we get him in it. Then he says in a strong deep voice I hardly recognize, "Arturo, get that notebook from the table, please."

I hand him another map-of-the-Island notebook—this one is red. On it in big letters it says, *POEMAS DE ARTURO.*

I start to push him toward the rec room, but he shakes his finger at me.

"Arturo, look at your watch now. I believe your time is over." He gives me a wicked smile.

Then with her pushing the wheelchair—maybe a little too fast—they roll down the hall. He is already reading from his notebook, and she's making bird noises. I look at my watch and the hour is up, to the minute. I can't help but think that my abuelo has been timing me. It cracks me up. I walk slowly down the hall toward the exit sign. I want my mother to have to wait a little. I don't want her to think that I'm in a hurry or anything.

About the Author

Judith Ortiz Cofer was born in Puerto Rico in 1952 and moved to New Jersey as a child. Since Spanish was her first language, she found it a challenge not only to learn English, but to master it, teach it, and ultimately write stories and poetry in it.

Responding to the Story

▼ Think Back

What reasons did Arturo give for not wanting to visit his abuelo?

What kind of person is Arturo? What kind of person is Abuelo? What details support your opinions?

Is Arturo's abuelo proud of his life? Explain.

▼ Discuss

Why didn't Arturo like the saying "*Así es la vida*"—that's the way life is? What is your opinion of the saying?

Arturo says "I can't help but think that my abuelo has been timing me." Why would Abuelo time Arturo?

What did Arturo learn about himself and his abuelo during his visit? Do you think he'll be more agreeable to visiting his abuelo in the future? Why or why not?

▼ Write

Write an Essay "An Hour With Abuelo" is written in informal language. Arturo tells the story as if he were talking to the reader. Write a brief essay describing a recent trip or experience. Use informal language.

Write Your Life Story Arturo's abuelo titled the story of his life *Así es la Vida*. What would you title your life story? Write a short story, similar to Abuelo's, describing your life. As you write, imagine that you are reading the story to someone.

Small Song for Daddy

W. D. Ehrhart

It isn't like my daughter

to awake at one a.m.—

but here she is.

This father doesn't care if his baby daughter wakes him at one in the morning. Why do her actions delight him?

She pulls the hairs on my chest

idly,[1] wiggles her toes, sighs

almost as if in meditation,[2]

and begins to sing softly,

[1] without purpose

[2] deep thought

the language hers alone,

the voice clear and fragile[3]

as water striking stone.

[3] delicate

New in a world where new

is all she knows, she sings

for each new wonder

she discovers—as if those

curtains, the chair, that

box of Kleenex were created

solely to delight her.

And they do. And she sings,

not knowing she is singing

for a father much in need

of her particular song.

About the Author

W. D. Ehrhart was born in 1948 in Roaring Spring, Pennsylvania. He has taught English, composition, and history and is the author of several books of poetry.

Responding to the Poem

▼ Think Back

This poem is about a daughter. How old do you think she is? What details give you clues about her age?

Is the daughter upset, or is she contented? How can you tell?

How does his daughter's "song" make the father feel?

▼ Discuss

What nonverbal cues, or body language, reveal the baby's feelings? What nonverbal cues might the father use to communicate his love for his daughter?

What advice would you give the father in the poem to help him continue to communicate effectively with his daughter as she grows?

▼ Write

Create Similes A simile uses the words *like* or *as* to compare two unlike things. In "Small Song for Daddy" W. D. Ehrhart compares the fragile sound of his daughter's voice to the sound of "water striking stone." Create a list of original similes that describe the voices of several people you know.

Write a Description The father in the poem focuses on describing his daughter's voice. Describe someone you admire or love. Use a variety of similes to focus on one characteristic, such as voice, eyes, or gestures.

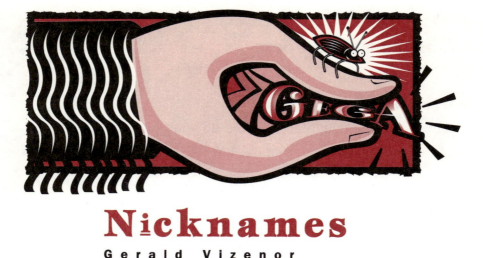

Nicknames

Gerald Vizenor

Some families like to use nicknames. Do you like the nicknames Uncle Clement chose?

U ncle Clement told me last night that he knows *almost* everything. Almost, that's his nickname and favorite word in stories, lives with me and my mother in a narrow house on the Leech Lake Chippewa Indian Reservation in northern Minnesota.

Last night, just before dark, we drove into town to meet my cousin at the bus depot and to buy rainbow ice cream in thick brown cones. Almost sat in the backseat of our old car and started his stories the minute we were on the dirt road around the north side of the lake to town. The wheels bounced and the car doors shuddered[1] and raised thick clouds of dust. He told me about the time he almost started an ice cream store when he came back from the army. My mother laughed and turned to the side. The car rattled on the washboard road. She shouted, "I heard that one before!"

"Almost!" he shouted back.

"What almost happened?" I asked. My voice bounced with the car.

[1] shook

"Well, it was winter then," he said. Fine brown dust settled on his head and the shoulders of his overcoat. "Too cold for ice cream in the woods, but the idea came to mind in the summer, almost."

"Almost, you know almost everything about nothing," my mother shouted and then laughed, "or almost nothing about almost everything."

"Pincher, we're almost to the ice cream," he said, and brushed me on the head with his hard right hand. He did that to ignore what my mother said about what he knows. Clouds of dust covered the trees behind us on both sides of the road.

I pinched animals, insects, leaves, water, fish, ice cream, the moist night air, winter breath, snow, and even words, the words I could see, or almost see.

Almost is my great-uncle and he decides on our nicknames, even the nicknames for my cousins who live in the cities and visit the reservation in the summer. Pincher, the name he gave me, was natural because I pinched my way through childhood. I learned about the world between two fingers. I pinched everything, or *almost* everything as my uncle would say. I pinched animals, insects, leaves, water, fish, ice cream, the moist night air, winter breath, snow, and even words, the words I could see, or almost see. I pinched the words and learned how to speak sooner than my cousins. Pinched words are easier to remember. Some words, like *government* and *grammar*, are unnatural, never seen and never pinched. Who could pinch a word like grammar?

Almost named me last winter when my grandmother was sick with pneumonia and died on the way to the public health hospital. She had no teeth and covered her mouth when she smiled, almost a child. I sat in the backseat of the car and held her thin brown hand. Even her veins were hidden, it was so cold that night. On the road we pinched summer words over the hard snow and ice. She smiled and said *papakine, papakine*, over and over. That means cricket or grasshopper in our tribal language and we pinched that word together. We pinched *papakine* in the backseat of our cold car on the way to the hospital. Later she whispered *bisanagami sibi*, the river is still, and then she died. My mother straightened my grandmother's fingers, but later, at the wake in our house, she'd pinched a summer word and we could see that. She was buried in the cold earth with a warm word between her fingers. That's when my uncle gave me my nickname.

Almost never told lies, but he used the word *almost* to stretch the truth like a tribal trickster, my mother told me. The trickster is a character in stories, an animal, or person, even a tree at times, who pretends the world can be stopped with words, and he frees the world in stories. Almost said the trickster is almost a man and almost a woman, and almost a child, a clown, who laughs and plays games with words in stories. The trickster is almost a free spirit. Almost told me about the trickster many times, and I think I almost understood his stories. He brushed my head with his hand and said, "The *almost* world is a better world, a sweeter dream than the world we are taught to understand in school."

"I understand, almost," I told my uncle.

"People are almost stories, and stories tell almost the whole truth," Almost told me last winter when he gave me my nickname. "Pincher is your nickname and names are stories too, *gega*." The word *gega* means almost in the Anishinaabe or Chippewa language.

"Pincher *gega*," I said, and then tried to pinch a tribal word I could not yet see clear enough to hold between my fingers. I could almost see *gega*.

About the Author

Gerald Vizenor, a mixed blood member of the Minnesota Chippewa Tribe, was born in 1934 in Minneapolis. He has written poetry as well as novels such as *Almost a Whole Trickster*, from which this excerpt was taken.

Responding to the Story

▼ Think Back

What does the narrator think of her Uncle Almost? What details give you clues about her feelings?

How did the narrator get the nickname Pincher?

How did the narrator's family react to the grandmother's death? Explain.

▼ Discuss

Almost said, "The *almost* world is a better world, a sweeter dream than the world we are taught to understand in school." What do you think he means? Do you think he is right?

Almost gave nicknames to everyone in the narrator's family. Why was it important for everyone to have a nickname? What purpose do nicknames serve?

▼ Write

Use Descriptive Language The author uses descriptive language. Find and read the passage describing the car ride to town. Then use descriptive language to write about a recent car ride you experienced.

Create Nicknames Do you have a nickname? In your opinion, is it an accurate description of you? Invent nicknames for some people you know. Use descriptive language to explain the reasons for your choices.

My Reputation

Arthur Ashe

I f one's reputation is a possession, then of all my possessions, my reputation means most to me. Nothing comes even close to it in importance. Now and then, I have wondered whether my reputation matters too much to me; but I can no more easily renounce[1] my concern with what other people think of me than I can will myself to stop breathing. No matter what I do, or where or when I do it, I feel the eyes of others on me, judging me.

Needless to say, I know that a fine line exists between caring about one's reputation and hypocrisy.[2] When I speak of the importance to me of my reputation, I am referring to a reputation that is deserved, not an image cultivated[3] for the public in spite of the facts. I know that I haven't always lived without error or sin, but I also know that I have tried hard to be honest and good at all times. When I fail, my conscience comes alive. I have never sinned or erred without knowing I was being watched.

Arthur Ashe was one of America's greatest tennis players. He lived by this motto: "A good name is worth more than diamonds and gold."

[1] give up or put aside

[2] the act of pretending to be what one is not

[3] trained and developed

Who is watching me? The living and the dead. My mother, Mattie Cordell Cunningham Ashe, watches me. She died when I was not quite seven. I remember little about her, except for two images. My last sight of her alive: I was finishing breakfast and she was standing in the side doorway looking lovingly at me. She was dressed in her blue corduroy dressing gown. The day was cool and cloudy, and when I went outside I heard birds singing in the small oak tree outside our house. And then I remember the last time I saw her, in a coffin at home. She was wearing her best dress, made of pink satin. In her right hand was a single red rose. Roses were her favorite flower, and my daddy had planted them all around the house; big, deep-hued red roses.

Every day since then I have thought about her. I would give anything to stand once again before her, to feel her arms about me, to touch and taste her skin. She is with me every day, watching me in everything I do. Whenever I speak to young persons about the morality[4] of the decisions they make in life, I usually tell them, "Don't do anything you couldn't tell your mother about."

My father is watching me, too. My father, whose mouth dropped open when he first saw Jeanne, my wife. She looked so much like my mother, he said. He is still a force in my life. Some years ago, before he died of a stroke in 1989, I was being interviewed by the television journalist Charlayne Hunter-Gault in her home.

"Tell me, Arthur," she said, laughter in her voice, "how is it that I have never heard anyone say anything bad about you? How is it that you have never cursed an

[4] rightness or wrongness

umpire, or punched an opponent,[5] or gotten a little drunk and disorderly? Why are you such a goody-goody?"

I laughed in turn, and told the truth.

"I guess I have never misbehaved because I'm afraid that if I did anything like that, my father would come straight up from Virginia, find me wherever I happen to be, and kick my ass."

When I told that story not long ago on Men's Day at the Westwood Baptist Church in Richmond, Virginia, everyone smiled and some folks even laughed. They knew what I was talking about, even those few living in that little enclave of blacks surrounded by whites in Richmond who had never met my father. They knew fathers (and mothers) exactly like him, who in times past would come up and find you wherever you were and remind you exactly who you were and don't you forget it. You were their child, that's who.

My father was a strong, dutiful, providing man. He lived and died semi-literate,[6] but he owned his own home and held jobs that were important to him and to people in the community where we lived. His love and his caring were real to me from that Sunday morning in 1950 when he sat on the bottom bunk bed between my brother Johnnie and me and told us between wrenching sobs that our mother had died during the night. From that time on he was father and mother to us. And the lesson he taught above all was about reputation.

"What people think of you, Arthur Junior, your reputation, is all that counts." Or, as I heard from so many older people as I grew up, "A good name is worth more than diamonds and gold."

What others think of me is important, and what I think of others is important. What else do I have to go by? Of course, I cannot make decisions based solely on what other people would think. There are moments when the individual must stand alone. Nevertheless, it is crucial[7] to me that people think of me as honest and principled. In turn, to ensure that they do, I must always act in an honest and principled fashion, no matter the cost.

One day, in Dallas, Texas, in 1973, I was playing in the singles final of a World Championship Tennis (WCT) tournament. My opponent was Stan Smith, a brilliant tennis player but an even more impressive human being in his integrity.[8] On one crucial point, I watched Smith storm forward, racing to intercept a ball about to bounce a second time on his side of the net. When the point was over, I was sure the ball had bounced twice before he hit it and that the point was mine. Smith said he had reached the ball in time. The umpire was baffled. The crowd was buzzing.

I called Smith up to the net.

"Stan, did you get to that ball?"

"I did. I got it."

I conceded[9] the point. Later, after the match—which I lost—a reporter approached me. Was I so naive?[10] How could I have taken Smith's word on such an important point?

[7] very important

[8] honesty and uprightness

[9] agreed to give something up
[10] believing; not suspicious

"Believe me," I assured him, "I am not a fool. I wouldn't take just anybody's word for it. But if Stan Smith says he got to the ball, he got to it. I trust his character."

When I was not quite eighteen years old, I played a tournament in Wheeling, West Virginia, the Middle Atlantic Junior Championships. As happened much of the time when I was growing up, I was the only black kid in the tournament, at least in the under-eighteen age section. One night, some of the other kids trashed a cabin; they absolutely destroyed it. And then they decided to say that I was responsible, although I had nothing to do with it. The incident even got into the papers. As much as I denied and protested, those white boys would not change their story.

I rode to Washington from West Virginia with the parents of Dickie Dell, another one of the players. They tried to reassure me, but it was an uncomfortable ride because I was silently worrying about what my father would do and say to me. When I reached Washington, where I was to play in another tournament, I telephoned him in Richmond. As I was aware, he already knew about the incident. When he spoke, he was grim. But he had one question only.

"Arthur Junior, all I want to know is, were you mixed up in that mess?"

"No, Daddy, I wasn't."

He never asked about it again. He trusted me. With my father, my reputation was solid.

I have tried to live so that people would trust my character, as I had trusted Stan Smith's. Sometimes I think it is almost a weakness in me, but I want to be seen as fair and honest, trustworthy, kind, calm, and polite. I want no stain on my character, no blemish on my reputation.

About the Author

Arthur Ashe (1943–1993) was one of the most famous tennis players in the world. He served as captain of the U.S. Davis Cup Team, and he became the first African American to win the U.S. Open. Ashe founded the Junior Tennis League, an organization that brought tennis instructors and young players together. He wrote several books about tennis and two autobiographies. He also wrote for the Washington *Post* and was a sports commentator for ABC television.

Responding to the Autobiography

▼ Think Back

Why does Arthur Ashe have such respect and love for his father?

What was the most important lesson Arthur Senior taught his son?

How would you describe the relationship between Arthur Ashe and his father? What details give you clues to how they felt about one another?

▼ Discuss

Arthur Ashe wanted a solid reputation that he deserved, not "an image cultivated for the public in spite of the facts." What did he mean?

What did you learn about Arthur Ashe from "My Reputation"? What else did you learn? Was Ashe trying to teach a lesson in this essay? Explain.

▼ Write

Record a Memorable Incident Arthur Ashe recalls the influence his parents had on his life and character. Think about a person who has influenced you. Write a detailed account of an incident that explains that influence.

Write an Essay What quality in your character is most important to you? Using specific incidents to support your ideas, write an essay similar to "My Reputation."

Theme Links

Families

In this unit, you've read about people and characters who live in a variety of family settings. You have also explored how relationships within families change as members grow and mature. Then you thought about your own family and what it means to you.

▼ Group Discussion

With a partner or in a small group, talk about the selections in this unit and how they relate to the theme and to your own lives. Use questions like the following to guide the discussion.

- What is special about the families in the selections in the unit?
- Which of these people might you want to adopt into your own family? Why?
- Which family is most similar to yours? Which family is most different from yours? Explain the similarities or differences.
- How do the selections in this unit point out the values, traits, and motivations that many families share?

▼ Hearing from the Characters

Imagine you are a person or character from one of the selections in this unit. Prepare a short speech that you could use to introduce the most influential relative in your life to the class.

▼ Talking About Babies

Bringing home a new baby is an important event in families. Imagine that Shirley Jackson's children met the father and the daughter from the poem "Small Song for Daddy." What advice do you think they might give to him? Write a conversation among them and then perform it for the class.

▼ Your Family

Make a scrapbook about your family. Choose photographs, memorabilia, and other family artifacts that document your life with your family. Write captions for the pictures and mementos explaining their significance. Include the following in your scrapbook:

- an autobiography
- photographs
- mementos
- family letters
- a copy of your family tree

▼ The Theme and You

What is special about the members of your family? Think about your parents, brothers and sisters, and other close relatives. Then make up a free-verse poem about your family by writing each person's name and then below it writing three pairs of verbs and adverbs that describe that person. For example, you might write this line for a younger brother.

> John
> runs fast, shares sometimes, jokes around

Memories

Do you take photographs? Do you keep a scrapbook, journal, or diary? Why is it important to record what happens in your life?

You, like most people, have memories that will be with you throughout your life. You might recall a brief moment or single event, or you might remember vividly an entire season or year. Your

memories are like a road map that shows where you've been in your life. What are your strongest memories?

The readings that follow describe powerful memories. Some are very personal. Others describe events that affected many people. As you read, think about what your memories tell you about yourself. How will your memories help future generations understand your time?

Concha

M a r y   H e l e n   P o n c e

This story may remind you of games you played as a child. How does Concha amaze her playmates?

[1] collected

While growing up in the small barrio of Pacoima my younger brother Joey and I were left alone to find ways *para divertirnos*, to keep ourselves busy—and out of our mother's way. One way in which we whiled away long summer days was by making pea shooters. These were made from a hollow reed which we first cleaned with a piece of wire. We then collected berries from *los pirules*, the pepper trees that lined our driveway. Once we amassed[1] enough dry berries we put them in our mouths and spat them out at each other through the pea shooter.

The berries had a terrible taste—they were even said to be poison! I was most careful not to swallow them. We selected only the hard, firm peas. The soft ones, we knew, would get mushy, crumble in our mouths and force us to gag—and lose a fight. During an important battle a short pause could spell defeat. Oftentimes while playing with Joey I watched closely. When he appeared to gag I dashed back to the pepper tree to load up on ammunition. I pelted him without mercy until he begged me to stop.

"No more. *Ya no*," Joey cried as he bent over to spit berries. "No more!"

"Ha, ha I got you now." I spat berries at Joey until, exhausted, we called a truce and slumped onto a wooden bench.

In fall our game came to a halt—the trees dried up; the berries fell to the ground. This was a sign for us to begin other games.

Our games were seasonal. During early spring we made whistles from the long blades of grass that grew in the open field behind our house. In winter we made dams, forts and canals from the soft mud that was our street. We tied burnt matchsticks together with string. These were our men. We positioned them along the forts (camouflaged[2] with small branches). We also played kick the can, but our most challenging game was playing with red ants.

[2] covered up; hidden

The ants were of the common variety: red, round and treacherous. They invaded our yard and the *llano*[3] every summer. We always knew where ants could be found, *donde habia ormigas*. We liked to build mud and grass forts smack in the middle of ant territory. The ants were the enemy, the matchstickmen the heroes, or good guys.

[3] *Spanish*: plain

Playing with ants was a real challenge! While placing our men in battle positions we timed it so as not to get bitten. We delighted in beating the ants at their own game.

Sometimes we got really brave and picked up ants with a stick, then twirled the stick around until the ants got dizzy-drunk (or so we thought)—and fell to the ground. We made ridges of dirt and pushed the ants inside, covered them with dirt and made bets as to how long it would take them to dig their way out.

Concha, my best friend and neighbor, was quite timid at school. She avoided all rough games such as kickball and Red Rover. When it came to playing with ants, however, Concha held first place for bravery. She could stand with her feet atop an anthill for the longest time! We stood trembling as ants crawled up our shoes, then quickly stomped our feet to scare them off. But Concha never lost her nerve.

One time we decided to have an ant contest. The prize was a candy bar—a Sugar Daddy sucker. We first found an anthill, lined up, then took turns standing beside the anthill while the juicy red ants climbed over our shoes. We dared not move—but when the first ant moved towards our ankles we stomped away, our Oxfords[4] making swirls of dust that allowed us to retreat to the sidelines. But not Concha. She remained in place as big red ants crept up her shoes. One, five, ten! We stood and counted, holding our breath as the ants continued to climb. Fifteen, twenty! Twenty ants were crawling over Concha!

"*Ujule*,[5] she sure ain't scared," cried Mundo in a hushed voice. "*No le tiene miedo a las ormigas*."

[4] sturdy shoes with laces

[5] *Spanish*: Oooh; Wow

"Uhhhhh," answered Beto, his eyes wide.

". . . I mean for a girl," added Mundo as he poked Beto in the ribs. We knew Beto liked Concha—and always came to her rescue.

We stood and counted ants. We were so caught up in this feat that we failed to notice the twenty-first ant that climbed up the back of Concha's sock . . . and bit her!

"Ay, ay, ay," screeched Concha.

"Gosh, she's gonna die," cried an alarmed Virgie as she helped stomp out ants. "She's gonna die!"

"She's too stupid to die," laughed Mundo, busy brushing ants off his feet. "She's too stupid."

"But sometimes people die when ants bite them," insisted Virgie, her face pale. "They gets real sick."

"The ants will probably die," Mundo snickered, holding his stomach and laughing loudly. "Ah, ha, ha."

"Gosh you're mean," said a shocked Virgie, hands on hips. "You are so mean."

"Yeah, but I ain't stupid."

**"The ants will probably die,"
Mundo snickered, holding his
stomach and laughing loudly.
"Ah, ha, ha."**

"Come on you guys, let's get her to the *mangera*," Beto cried as he reached out to Concha who by now had decided she would live. "Come on, let's take her to the faucet."

We held Concha by the waist as she hobbled to the water faucet. Her cries were now mere whimpers as no grownup had come out to investigate.[6] From experience we knew that if a first cry did not bring someone to our aid we should stop crying—or go home.

We helped Concha to the faucet, turned it on and began to mix water with dirt. We knew the best remedy for insect bites was *lodo*. We applied mud to all bug stings to stop the swelling. Mud was especially good for wasp stings, the yellowjackets we so feared—and from which we ran away at top speed. Whenever bees came close we stood still until they flew away, but there were no set rules on how to get rid of *avispas*. We hit out at them, and tried to scare them off but the yellowjackets were fierce! In desperation[7] we flung dirt at them, screamed and ran home.

Not long after the ant incident Concha decided she was not about to run when a huge wasp broke up our game of jacks. She stood still, so still the wasp remained on her dark head for what seemed like hours. We stood and watched, thinking perhaps the wasp had mistaken Concha's curly hair for a bush! We watched—and waited.

"*Ujule*, she sure is brave," exclaimed Virgie as she sucked on a popsicle. "She sure is brave."

"She's stupid," grunted Mundo, trying to be indifferent. "She's just a big show-off who thinks she's so big."

"So are you," began Virgie, backing off. "So are you."

"Yeah? Ya wanna make something outta it?"

"Let's go," interrupted Beto in his soft voice. "*Ya vamonos*." He smiled at Concha—who smiled back.

In time the wasp flew away. Concha immediately began to brag about how a "real big wasp" sat on her hair for hours. She never mentioned the ant contest—nor the twenty-first ant that led her to *el lodo*.

About the Author

Mary Helen Ponce was born in 1938 in Pacoima, California. Ponce married and had a family immediately after graduating from high school. When her youngest son started school in 1974, Ponce resumed her own education, going on to earn several degrees and to teach at the college level. She loves to write as well as study history and literature. Her published works include a collection of short stories, *Taking Control*; a novel, *The Wedding*; and her autobiography, *Hoyt Street*. Ponce has said that "Concha" is autobiographical. The title character is a composite of two of her childhood friends.

Responding to the Story

▼ Think Back

What games did the narrator and her friends play?

How would you describe the narrator and her friends? What details help you form your opinions?

Did everyone admire Concha? Explain.

▼ Discuss

As children, the narrator and her friends created their own fun and games. Children today have many toys to choose from and many forms of entertainment. In your opinion, is it better for kids to invent their own entertainment? Why or why not?

The narrator wrote that Concha was timid and that she avoided rough games. Why would Concha play games with ants and other insects where she often put herself in physical danger?

▼ Write

Informal Speech The dialogue in "Concha" contains words and phrases that the narrator and her friends used. This helps make the story more authentic and more descriptive. Make a list of words and phrases that you and your friends use every day.

Use Dialogue Think of a memorable event in your life that happened several years ago. Write a short description of the event. Use dialogue to make it come alive.

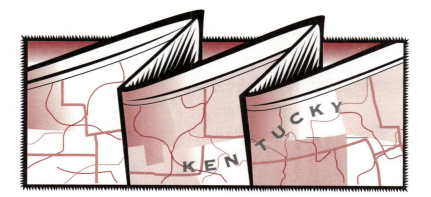

Everette Tharp's
Memories of Appalachia

Guy and Candie Carawan

I was born on June the thirteenth, 1899, in eastern Kentucky. I was raised on a farm with domestic and wild animals. Sheep, hogs, and cattle roamed wild in the forest. We raised what we ate and slept in dilapidated[1] houses. We enjoyed nature in all of its aspects and knew no doctors or surgeons. Mountain dew[2] was our principal medicine.

I knew the whistle of the ground hog, the call of the crow, the songs of the birds, the cunning of the fox, and the squall of the bobcat. I knew the art and expertise[3] of teaching an oxen to put his neck to the yoke and to kneel down low when his load was too heavy. These are things that can't be taught in the classroom.

The mountains of eastern Kentucky were a vast domain, rich in the abundance of nature to sustain domestic and wild animals. The timberlands, valleys, mountains, and streams were a Garden of Eden where the lamb lay down with the lion. There were no barbed-wire fences to restrain men. The mountain man knew how, as

Appalachia is a region of the United States that extends from West Virginia and southeast Ohio to northern Georgia. One man recalls what life was like there about 100 years ago.

[1] broken down; shabby

[2] homemade whiskey

[3] expert opinion or knowledge

the Indian did, to live off the land. At this time there were no phonographs, no radios, no television, no automobiles, no railroads, no public highways, no airplanes. Our highways were buffalo trails made by wild animals and later on used by the Indians and white adventurers. Freight boats traveled the Kentucky River to transport the necessaries of life to Hazard and Whitesburg.

I lived through the aftermath of the mountain feuds when father was committed against son and brother against brother. I lived by the code of the mountains. I lived in an age when people respected honor and truth, where a liar was scorned and ridiculed and a man who would not pay his debts was considered an outcast.

When the railroad pushed up the valley from Jackson to Hazard and on to McRoberts, it marked the beginning of the end of a way of life for a group of rugged men and women who had the nerve and the courage to traverse[4] the mountain barriers and establish rugged individualism[5]—known as the "mountain man way of life."

[4] to travel across

[5] act of leading life in one's own way

About the Author

Guy and Candie Carawan's *Voices from the Mountains* is a collection of songs, interviews, and stories about Appalachia. The Carawans were active in the civil rights movement and edited *We Shall Overcome* and *Freedom Is a Constant Struggle*.

Responding to the Essay

▼ Think Back

What was life like in Appalachia in the early 1900s?

What brought about the beginning of the end to the way of life Everette Tharp describes?

What is Tharp's opinion of Appalachia and the "mountain man" way of life?

▼ Discuss

Tharp stated, "I lived in an age when people respected honor and truth, where a liar was scorned and ridiculed and a man who would not pay his debts was considered an outcast." Have people today lost respect for honor and truth, as Tharp seems to be suggesting? Explain.

What aspects of the "mountain man" way of life do you find appealing?

▼ Write

List Details By using specific details, Everette Tharp makes his "story" more interesting and clear. He tells of the "whistle of the ground hog, the songs of the birds," and so on. Create a list of details about your childhood. What animals were around you? What did you do for fun? What was your neighborhood like?

Write an Essay Write an essay similar to Tharp's that describes your childhood. Use specific details from your list to support your points.

Seeing Snow

Gustavo Pérez-Firmat

Have you ever felt that you belong somewhere else? This poet asks himself, "What am I doing here?"

Had my father, my grandfather, and his,

had they been asked whether I would ever see snow,

they certainly—in another language—

would have answered

no. Seeing snow for me

will always mean a slight or not so slight

suspension[1] of the laws of nature.

I was not born to see snow.

I was not meant to see snow.

Even now, snowbound as I've been

all these years,

[1] temporary stoppage

my surprise does not subside.[2]

What, exactly, am I doing here?

Whose house is this anyway?

For sure one of us has strayed.

For sure someone's lost his way.

This must not be the place.

Where I come from, you know,

it's never snowed:

not once, not ever, not yet.

[2] become less active or intense

About the Author

Gustavo Pérez-Firmat was born in Cuba in 1949 and moved to Miami in 1960. He earned a Ph.D. at the University of Michigan. He is a critic as well as a professor of Spanish language and literature at Duke University in North Carolina. Pérez-Firmat writes in Spanish, his mother tongue; English, his other tongue; and in combinations of the two. He has written two books of poetry, *Carolina Cuban* and *Bilingual Blues*.

Responding to the Poem

▼ Think Back

Why does the speaker call his seeing snow a "suspension of the laws of nature"?

Where do you think the speaker is from? Where is he living now? On what details do you base your opinions?

What feelings or emotions does the speaker show in this poem?

▼ Discuss

In your opinion, what would the speaker's father, grandfather, and great grandfather say to him if they had the opportunity?

The speaker asks the questions, "What, exactly, am I doing here?" and "Whose house is this anyway?" What do these questions mean?

▼ Write

Identify the Theme The key idea or meaning of a work of literature is called its theme. Reread "Seeing Snow" and identify what you think is its theme. In a paragraph or two, describe the theme of the poem.

Write a Poem Think about the poems you read earlier. What are some of the themes in those poems? Does one theme appeal to you or catch your interest? Write a poem that is built around that theme.

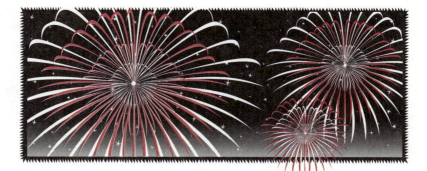

Day of the Refugios

Alberto Ríos

I was born in Nogales, Arizona,
On the border between
Mexico and the United States.

The places in between places
They are like little countries
Themselves, with their own holidays

Taken a little from everywhere.
My Fourth of July is from childhood,
Childhood itself a kind of country, too.

It's a place that's far from me now,
A place I'd like to visit again.
The Fourth of July always takes me there.

In that childhood place and border place
The Fourth of July, like everything else,
It meant more than just one thing.

Most of us have a favorite holiday. What's special about this family's Fourth of July?

In the United States the Fourth of July
It was the United States.
In Mexico it was the *día de los Refugios*,

The saint's day of people named Refugio.
I come from a family of people with names,
Real names, not-afraid names, with colors

Like the fireworks: Refugio,
Margarito, Matilde, Alvaro, Consuelo,
Humberto, Olga, Celina, Gilberto.

Names that take a moment to say,
Names you have to practice.
These were the names of saints, serious ones.

And it was right to take a moment with them.
I guess that's what my family thought.
The connection to saints was strong:

My grandmother's name—here it comes—
Her name was Refugio,
And my great-grandmother's name was Refugio,

And my mother-in-law's name now,
It's another Refugio, Refugios everywhere,
Refugios and shrimp cocktails and sodas.

Fourth of July was a birthday party
For all the women in my family
Going way back, a party

For everything Mexico, where they came from,
For the other words and the green
Tinted glasses my great-grandmother wore.

These women were me,
What I was before me,
So that birthday fireworks in the evening,

All for them,
This seemed right.
In that way the fireworks were for me, too.

Still, we were in the United States now,
And the Fourth of July,
Well, it was the Fourth of July.

But just what that meant,
In this border place and time,
It was a matter of opinion in my family.

About the Author

Alberto Ríos, a poet and short story writer, was born in 1952 in Nogales, Arizona, a town on the United States border with Mexico. Having a Mexican father and an English mother, Ríos says, "I grew up on the border in regards to all kinds of metaphorical borders: in between countries, languages, cultures, decades." Ríos also says that he "writes often about this, especially the Mexican/Chicano aspects."

Responding to the Poem

▼ Think Back

Why does the speaker think Refugio is a good name?

What does the speaker think of her heritage? What details support your opinion?

Why was the Fourth of July/*día de los Refugios* important to the speaker?

▼ Discuss

The poem's speaker says, "I come from a family of people with names, Real names, not-afraid names, with colors . . ." What do you think she means?

In your opinion, what is more important to the speaker and her family—celebrating the Fourth of July, or celebrating *día de los Refugios*? Explain.

▼ Write

Identify Mood Poet Alberto Ríos creates a mood of celebration and magic with his choice of words. Reread the poem and locate words or phrases that contribute to this celebratory mood. In a brief summary, explain how each example contributes to the mood.

Write a Poem Is there a holiday that stirs fond memories of your childhood? Using "Day of the Refugios" as a model, write a poem describing what that holiday means to you. Use words and phrases that capture your feelings and the mood of that day.

Two Kinds
from *The Joy Luck Club*

A m y   T a n

Every night after dinner, my mother and I would sit at the Formica kitchen table. She would present new tests, taking her examples from stories of amazing children she had read in *Ripley's Believe It or Not*, or *Good Housekeeping*, *Readers Digest*, and a dozen other magazines she kept in a pile in our bathroom. My mother got these magazines from people whose houses she cleaned. And since she cleaned many houses each week, we had a great assortment. She would look through them all, searching for stories about remarkable children.

The first night she brought out a story about a three-year-old boy who knew the capitals of all the states and even most of the European countries. A teacher was quoted as saying the little boy could also pronounce the names of the foreign cities correctly.

"What's the capital of Finland?" my mother asked me, looking at the magazine story.

All I knew was the capital of California, because Sacramento was the name of the street we lived on in

> Jing-mei's mother says that there are only two kinds of daughters. Which kind of daughter is Jing-mei?

Chinatown. "Nairobi!" I guessed, saying the most foreign word I could think of. She checked to see if that was possibly one way to pronounce "Helsinki" before showing me the answer.

The tests got harder—multiplying numbers in my head, finding the queen of hearts in a deck of cards, trying to stand on my head without using my hands, predicting the daily temperatures in Los Angeles, New York, and London.

One night I had to look at a page from the Bible for three minutes and then report everything I could remember. "Now Jehoshaphat had riches and honor in abundance and. . . that's all I remember, Ma," I said.

And after seeing my mother's disappointed face once again, something inside of me began to die. I hated the tests, the raised hopes and failed expectations. Before going to bed that night, I looked in the mirror above the bathroom sink and when I saw only my face staring back—and that it would always be this ordinary face—I began to cry. Such a sad, ugly girl! I made high-pitched noises like a crazed animal, trying to scratch out the face in the mirror.

And then I saw what seemed to be the prodigy[1] side of me—because I had never seen that face before. I looked at my reflection, blinking so I could see more clearly. The girl staring back at me was angry, powerful. This girl and I were the same. I had new thoughts, willful thoughts, or rather thoughts filled with lots of won'ts. I won't let her change me, I promised myself. I won't be what I'm not.

[1] very talented young person

So now on nights when my mother presented her tests, I performed listlessly,[2] my head propped on one arm. I pretended to be bored. And I was. I got so bored I started counting the bellows of the foghorns out on the bay while my mother drilled me in other areas. The sound was comforting and reminded me of the cow jumping over the moon. And the next day, I played a game with myself, seeing if my mother would give up on me before eight bellows. After a while I usually counted only one, maybe two bellows at most. At last she was beginning to give up hope.

Two or three months had gone by without any mention of my being a prodigy again. And then one day my mother was watching *The Ed Sullivan Show* on TV. The TV was old and the sound kept shorting out. Every time my mother got halfway up from the sofa to adjust the set, the sound would go back on and Ed would be talking. As soon as she sat down, Ed would go silent again. She got up, the TV broke into loud piano music. She sat down. Silence. Up and down, back and forth, quiet and loud. It was like a stiff embraceless dance between her and the TV set. Finally she stood by the set with her hand on the sound dial.

She seemed entranced[3] by the music, a little frenzied[4] piano piece with this mesmerizing[5] quality, sort of quick passages and then teasing lilting ones before it returned to the quick playful parts.

"*Ni kan*," my mother said, calling me over with hurried hand gestures, "Look here."

[2] without interest or enthusiasm

[3] under the spell of

[4] wild

[5] bewitching

I could see why my mother was fascinated by the music. It was being pounded out by a little Chinese girl, about nine years old, with a Peter Pan haircut. The girl had the sauciness of a Shirley Temple. She was proudly modest like a proper Chinese child. And she also did this fancy sweep of a curtsy, so that the fluffy skirt of her white dress cascaded[6] slowly to the floor like the petals of a large carnation.

6 flowed

In spite of these warning signs, I wasn't worried. Our family had no piano and we couldn't afford to buy one, let alone reams of sheet music and piano lessons. So I could be generous in my comments when my mother bad-mouthed the little girl on TV.

"Play note right, but doesn't sound good! No singing sound," complained my mother.

"What are you picking on her for?" I said carelessly. "She's pretty good. Maybe she's not the best, but she's trying hard." I knew almost immediately I would be sorry I said that.

"Just like you," she said. "Not the best. Because you not trying." She gave a little huff as she let go of the sound dial and sat down on the sofa.

The little Chinese girl sat down also to play an encore of "Anitra's Dance" by Grieg. I remember the song, because later on I had to learn how to play it.

Three days after watching *The Ed Sullivan Show*, my mother told me what my schedule would be for piano lessons and piano practice. She had talked to Mr. Chong, who lived on the first floor of our apartment building.

Mr. Chong was a retired piano teacher and my mother had traded housecleaning services for weekly lessons and a piano for me to practice on every day, two hours a day, from four until six.

When my mother told me this, I felt as though I had been sent to hell. I whined and then kicked my foot a little when I couldn't stand it anymore.

"Why don't you like me the way I am? I'm *not* a genius! I can't play the piano. And even if I could, I wouldn't go on TV if you paid me a million dollars!" I cried.

My mother slapped me. "Who ask you be genius?" she shouted. "Only ask you be your best. For you sake. You think I want you be genius? Hnnh! What for! Who ask you!"

"So ungrateful," I heard her mutter in Chinese. "If she had as much talent as she has temper, she would be famous now."

Mr. Chong, whom I secretly nicknamed Old Chong, was very strange, always tapping his fingers to the silent music of an invisible orchestra. He looked ancient in my eyes. He had lost most of the hair on top of his head and he wore thick glasses and had eyes that always looked tired and sleepy. But he must have been younger than I thought, since he lived with his mother and was not yet married.

I met Old Lady Chong once and that was enough. She had this peculiar smell like a baby that had done something in its pants. And her fingers felt like a dead person's, like an old peach I once found in the back of the refrigerator; the skin just slid off the meat when I picked it up.

I soon found out why Old Chong had retired from teaching piano. He was deaf. "Like Beethoven!" he shouted to me. "We're both listening only in our head!" And he would start to conduct his frantic silent sonatas.[7]

[7] musical pieces in several parts

Our lessons went like this. He would open the book and point to different things, explaining their purpose: "Key! Treble! Bass! No sharps or flats! So this is C major! Listen now and play after me!"

And then he would play the C scale a few times, a simple chord, and then, as if inspired by an old, unreachable itch, he gradually added more notes and running trills and a pounding bass until the music was really something quite grand.

I would play after him, the simple scale, the simple chord, and then I just played some nonsense that sounded like a cat running up and down on top of garbage cans. Old Chong smiled and applauded and then said, "Very good! But now you must learn to keep time!"

So that's how I discovered that Old Chong's eyes were too slow to keep up with the wrong notes I was playing. He went through the motions in half-time. To help me keep rhythm, he stood behind me, pushing down on my right shoulder for every beat. He balanced pennies on top of my wrists so I would keep them still as I slowly played scales and arpeggios.[8] He had me curve my hand around an apple and keep that shape when playing chords. He marched stiffly to show me

[8] notes of a chord played one by one

how to make each finger dance up and down, staccato[9] like an obedient little soldier.

[9] with a regular, sharp beat

He taught me all these things, and that was how I also learned I could be lazy and get away with mistakes, lots of mistakes. If I hit the wrong notes because I hadn't practiced enough, I never corrected myself. I just kept playing in rhythm. And Old Chong kept conducting his own private reverie.

So maybe I never really gave myself a fair chance. I did pick up the basics pretty quickly, and I might have became a good pianist at that young age. But I was so determined not to try, not to be anybody different that I learned to play only the most ear-splitting preludes,[10] the most discordant[11] hymns.

[10] introductory parts of musical pieces
[11] sour-sounding; inharmonious

Over the next year, I practiced like this, dutifully in my own way. And then one day I heard my mother and her friend Lindo Jong both talking in a loud bragging tone of voice so others could hear. It was after church, and I was leaning against the brick wall wearing a dress with stiff white petticoats. Auntie Lindo's daughter, Waverly, who was about my age, was standing farther down the wall about five feet away. We had grown up together and shared all the closeness of two sisters squabbling over crayons and dolls. In other words, for the most part, we hated each other. I thought she was snotty. Waverly Jong had gained a certain amount of fame as "Chinatown's Littlest Chinese Chess Champion."

"She bring home too many trophy," lamented Auntie Lindo that Sunday. "All day she play chess. All day I have no time do nothing but dust off her winnings." She threw a scolding look at Waverly, who pretended not to see her.

"You lucky you don't have this problem," said Auntie Lindo with a sigh to my mother.

And my mother squared her shoulders and bragged: "Our problem worser than yours. If we ask Jing-mei wash dish, she hear nothing but music. It's like you can't stop this natural talent."

And right then, I was determined to put a stop to her foolish pride.

A few weeks later, Old Chong and my mother conspired to have me play in a talent show which would be held in the church hall. By then, my parents had saved up enough to buy me a secondhand piano, a black Wurlitzer spinet with a scarred bench. It was the showpiece of our living room.

For the talent show, I was to play a piece called "Pleading Child" from Schumann's *Scenes from Childhood*. It was a simple, moody piece that sounded more difficult than it was. I was supposed to memorize the whole thing, playing the repeat parts twice to make the piece sound longer. But I dawdled over it, playing a few bars and then cheating, looking up to see what notes followed. I never really listened to what I was playing. I daydreamed about being somewhere else, about being someone else.

The part I liked to practice best was the fancy curtsy: right foot out, touch the rose on the carpet with a pointed foot, sweep to the side, left leg bends, look up and smile.

My parents invited all the couples from the Joy Luck Club to witness my debut. Auntie Lindo and Uncle Tin were there. Waverly and her two older brothers had also come. The first two rows were filled with children both younger and older than I was. The littlest ones got to go first. They recited simple nursery rhymes, squawked out tunes on miniature violins, twirled Hula Hoops, pranced in pink ballet tutus, and when they bowed or curtsied, the audience would sigh in unison, "Aww," and then clap enthusiastically.

When my turn came, I was very confident. I remember my childish excitement. It was as if I knew, without a doubt, that the prodigy side of me really did exist. I had no fear whatsoever, no nervousness. I remember thinking to myself, This is it! This is it! I looked out over the audience, at my mother's blank face, my father's yawn, Auntie Lindo's stiff-lipped smile, Waverly's sulky expression. I had on a white dress layered in sheets of lace, and a pink bow in my Peter Pan haircut. As I sat down I envisioned[12] people jumping to their feet and Ed Sullivan rushing up to introduce me to everyone on TV.

[12] pictured

And I started to play. It was so beautiful. I was so caught up in how lovely I looked that at first I didn't worry how I would sound. So it was a surprise to me when I hit the first wrong note and I realized something didn't sound quite right. And then I hit another and another followed that. A chill started at the top of my head and began to trickle down. Yet I couldn't stop playing, as though my hands were bewitched. I kept thinking my fingers would adjust themselves back, like a train switching to the right track. I played this strange jumble through two repeats, the sour notes staying with me all the way to the end.

When I stood up, I discovered my legs were shaking. Maybe I had just been nervous and the audience, like Old Chong, had seen me go through the right motions and had not heard anything wrong at all. I swept my right foot out, went down on my knee, looked up and smiled. The room was quiet, except for Old Chong, who was beaming and shouting, "Bravo! Bravo! Well done!" But then I saw my mother's face, her stricken face. The audience clapped weakly, and as I walked back to my chair, with my whole face quivering as I tried not to cry, I heard a little boy whisper loudly to his mother, "That was awful," and the mother whispered back, "Well, she certainly tried."

And now I realized how many people were in the audience, the whole world it seemed. I was aware of eyes burning into my back. I felt the shame of my mother and father as they sat stiffly throughout the rest of the show.

We could have escaped during intermission. Pride and some strange sense of honor must have anchored my parents to their chairs. And so we watched it all: the eighteen-year-old boy with a fake mustache who did a magic show and juggled flaming hoops while riding a unicycle. The breasted girl with white makeup who sang from *Madama Butterfly* and got honorable mention. And the eleven-year-old boy who won first prize playing a tricky violin song that sounded like a busy bee.

After the show, the Hsus, the Jongs, and the St. Clairs from the Joy Luck Club came up to my mother and father.

"Lots of talented kids," Auntie Lindo said vaguely, smiling broadly.

"That was somethin' else," said my father, and I wondered if he was referring to me in a humorous way, or whether he even remembered what I had done.

Waverly looked at me and shrugged her shoulders. "You aren't a genius like me," she said matter-of-factly. And if I hadn't felt so bad, I would have pulled her braids and punched her stomach.

But my mother's expression was what devastated[13] me: a quiet, blank look that said she had lost everything. I felt the same way, and it seemed as if everybody were now coming up, like gawkers at the scene of an accident, to see what parts were actually missing. When we got on the bus to go home, my father was humming the busy-bee tune and my mother was silent. I kept thinking she wanted to wait until we got home before shouting at me. But when my father unlocked the door to our apartment, my mother walked in and then went to the back, into the bedroom. No accusations. No blame. And in a way, I felt disappointed. I had been waiting for her to start shouting, so I could shout back and cry and blame her for all my misery.

I assumed my talent-show fiasco meant I never had to play the piano again. But two days later, after

[13] destroyed

school, my mother came out of the kitchen and saw me watching TV.

"Four clock," she reminded me as if it were any other day. I was stunned, as though she were asking me to go through the talent-show torture again. I wedged myself more tightly in front of the TV.

"Turn off TV," she called from the kitchen five minutes later.

I didn't budge. And then I decided. I didn't have to do what my mother said anymore. I wasn't her slave. This wasn't China. I had listened to her before and look what happened. She was the stupid one.

She came out from the kitchen and stood in the arched entryway of the living room. "Four clock," she said once again, louder.

"I'm not going to play anymore," I said nonchalantly.[14] "Why should I? I'm not a genius."

She walked over and stood in front of the TV. I saw her chest was heaving up and down in an angry way.

"No!" I said, and I now felt stronger, as if my true self had finally emerged. So this was what had been inside me all along.

"No! I won't!" I screamed.

She yanked me by the arm, pulled me off the floor, snapped off the TV. She was frighteningly strong, half pulling, half carrying me toward the piano as I kicked the throw rugs under my feet. She lifted me up and onto the hard bench. I was sobbing by now, looking at her bitterly. Her chest was heaving even more and her

[14] coolly, showing no emotion

mouth was open, smiling crazily as if she were pleased I was crying.

"You want me to be someone that I'm not!" I sobbed. "I'll never be the kind of daughter you want me to be!"

"Only two kinds of daughters," she shouted in Chinese. "Those who are obedient and those who follow their own mind! Only one kind of daughter can live in this house. Obedient daughter!"

"Then I wish I wasn't your daughter. I wish you weren't my mother," I shouted. As I said these things I got scared. It felt like worms and toads and slimy things crawling out of my chest, but it also felt good, as if this awful side of me had surfaced at last.

"Too late change this," said my mother shrilly.

And I could sense her anger rising to its breaking point. I wanted to see it spill over. and that's when I remembered the babies she had lost in China, the ones we never talked about. "Then I wish I'd never been born!" I shouted. "I wish I were dead! Like them."

It was as if I had said the magic words. Alakazam!—and her face went blank, her mouth closed, her arms went slack, and she backed out of the room, stunned, as if she were blowing away like a small brown leaf, thin, brittle, lifeless.

It was not the only disappointment my mother felt in me. In the years that followed, I failed her so many times, each time asserting my own will, my right to fall short of expectations. I didn't get straight As. I didn't

become class president. I didn't get into Stanford.
I dropped out of college.

For unlike my mother, I did not believe I could
be anything I wanted to be. I could only be me.

And for all those years, we never talked about the
disaster at the recital or my terrible accusations
afterward at the piano bench. All that remained
unchecked, like a betrayal that was now unspeakable. So
I never found a way to ask her why she had hoped for
something so large that failure was inevitable.[15]

And even worse, I never asked her what
frightened me the most: Why had she given up hope?

For after our struggle at the piano, she never
mentioned my playing again. The lessons stopped. The
lid to the piano was closed, shutting out the dust, my
misery, and her dreams.

So she surprised me. A few years ago, she offered
to give me the piano, for my thirtieth birthday. I had not
played in all those years. I saw the offer as a sign of
forgiveness, a tremendous burden removed.

"Are you sure?" I asked shyly. "I mean, won't you
and Dad miss it?"

"No, this your piano," she said firmly. "Always
your piano. You only one can play."

"Well, I probably can't play anymore," I said. "It's
been years."

"You pick up fast," said my mother, as if she
knew this was certain. "You have natural talent. You
could been genius if you want to."

"No I couldn't."

"You just not trying," said my mother. And she was neither angry nor sad. She said it as if to announce a fact that could never be disproved. "Take it," she said.

But I didn't at first. It was enough that she had offered it to me. And after that, every time I saw it in my parents' living room, standing in front of the bay windows, it made me feel proud, as if it were a shiny trophy I had won back.

Last week I sent a tuner over to my parents' apartment and had the piano reconditioned, for purely sentimental reasons. My mother had died a few months before and I had been getting things in order for my father, a little bit at a time. I put the jewelry in special silk pouches. The sweaters she had knitted in yellow, pink, bright orange—all the colors I hated—I put those in moth-proof boxes. I found some old Chinese silk dresses, the kind with little slits up the sides. I rubbed the old silk against my skin, then wrapped them in tissue and decided to take them home with me.

After I had the piano tuned, I opened the lid and touched the keys. It sounded even richer than I remembered. Really, it was a very good piano. Inside the bench were the same exercise notes with handwritten scales, the same secondhand music books with their covers held together with yellow tape.

I opened up the Schumann book to the dark little piece I had played at the recital. It was on the left-hand side of the page, "Pleading Child." It looked more difficult than I remembered. I played a few bars, surprised at how easily the notes came back to me.

And for the first time, or so it seemed, I noticed the piece on the right-hand side. It was called "Perfectly Contented." I tried to play this one as well. It had a lighter melody but the same flowing rhythm and turned out to be quite easy. "Pleading Child" was shorter but slower; "Perfectly Contented" was longer, but faster. And after I played them both a few times, I realized they were two halves of the same song.

About the Author

Amy Tan was born in Oakland, California, in 1952. Tan's work highlights and explores the gaps between generations as well as those between cultures. When she was young, her biculturalism confused her. Her parents had come from China and urged her to learn English. She found it hard to do this and remain Chinese. When she visited China for the first time in 1987, Tan said, "As soon as my feet touched China, I became Chinese." She won several awards for her first novel, *The Joy Luck Club*, from which this excerpt is taken. The novel was inspired by her desire to explore her relationship with her mother and her Chinese culture.

Responding to the Story

▼ Think Back

At the beginning of the story, the daughter was excited about becoming a prodigy. What made her lose her enthusiasm?

What were some of the reasons why the daughter didn't improve as a pianist?

What did the daughter say to end the argument about piano practice? What effect did it have on the mother?

▼ Discuss

What could the mother have done to make her daughter feel less pressured? What could the daughter have done to seem less stubborn and disobedient?

Reread the final paragraph. What does the daughter discover? What has she learned about herself?

▼ Write

Write an Essay Think of a conflict that you had with a parent or other adult when you were a child. What was each person's point of view on the issue? Write a brief essay in which you explain the conflict and compare the two points of view. Has your view changed since then?

Change the Point of View How would "Two Kinds" be different if the mother had told the story? Write several paragraphs about the piano lessons and talent show from the mother's point of view.

Theme Links

Memories

You've just read about vivid memories that some people have held onto for their entire lives. You discussed memories that involve personal experiences and memories that involve the lives of many people. You have also explored what your own memories tell you about yourself.

▼ Group Discussion

With a partner or in a small group, talk about the selections in this unit and how they relate to the theme and to your own lives. Use questions like the following to guide the discussion.

- What is special about the people or characters in these selections?
- Which character would you like to meet? Why?
- Which memories are especially moving or interesting?
- After reading the selections in this unit, what childhood memories of yours come to mind?

▼ This Is Your Life

In a small group, pick a character from one of the selections to be the guest on the "This Is Your Life" show. Prepare by reviewing the selection and noting the key people in the guest's life. Why were they important? What would they say to the guest? What memories would they talk about? Assign roles and perform your show for the class.

▼ Making Memories

Some of the memories you read about in these selections were happy ones, and some of them were unpleasant. It seems that we remember the high points and low points in our lives and forget much of the in between. Start a memory box for yourself. Begin by decorating an old shoe box with drawings or photos of things that represent favorite memories for you. At the end of each day write your favorite memory of the day on a small piece of paper, fold it up, and place it in the box. On a day when you don't have a good memory to write down, take an old one from the box and read it!

▼ The Theme and You

When you think back on your childhood, what memories come to mind? Who else is in those memories? Choose your most vivid childhood memory. Then write a letter to another person who shares that memory, telling her or him how you feel about it.

Surprises

When is an orange not an orange? The answer to that riddle is one of the many surprises you will find in the selections in this unit.

Can you think of times when you have been surprised—times when things turned out completely differently than you expected? How did you feel? Were you in shock? Were you happy? Were you sad?

Were you afraid? Surprises can cause many emotions, and they can teach people to look closely at situations before they come to a conclusion.

As you read these selections, be prepared for the unexpected. Put yourself in the place of the characters. What would you do if you were in their situations?

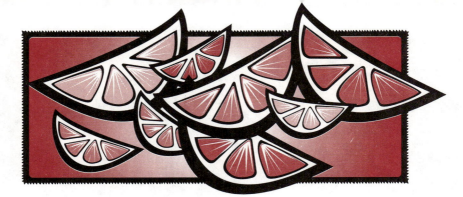

My Sister Ate an Orange

Jack Prelutsky

The girl in this poem
likes oranges. But
maybe she'd be
smarter eating apples
or bananas!

[1] causing worry

My sister ate an orange,
I'm astonished that she did,
she swallowed it completely,
she's a disconcerting[1] kid.

My sister ate an orange,
first she chewed it for awhile,
then digested it entirely
with a silly sort of smile.

My sister ate an orange,
it's a novel thing to do,
then she also ate a yellow
and a purple and a blue.

About the Author

**Jack Prelutsky first studied music and the visual arts
and later illustrated a book of his own poems. A publisher
recognized Prelutsky's talent for poetry, and he has since
written more than 30 poetry collections.**

Responding to the Poem

▼ Think Back

What is it that you first think the sister ate? Why did you think that?

What did the sister eat?

What does the speaker think of his sister's actions?

▼ Discuss

What makes this poem clever?

What do you think was the poet's purpose for writing this poem?

In your opinion, should all poems be about important or serious ideas? What purpose do humorous poems such as "My Sister Ate an Orange" serve?

▼ Write

Rhyme It A common poetry device is *rhyme*. Notice how and where Jack Prelutsky uses rhyme in this poem. Try changing the poem by writing new rhymes.

Write a Poem Write a silly or humorous poem about one of your relatives. Can you make it surprising? Use Prelutsky's rhyme scheme in "My Sister Ate an Orange" or invent your own.

Speed Cleen

James Stevenson

A man who stops at a car wash is in for a surprise. Find out why he'll probably wish that he'd washed the car himself!

[1] worker

[2] clothing or equipment no longer needed by the Army

Don't forget those little ashtrays in the back, my friend!" called Harry Joe Shreve, holding open the front door of his white Chrysler Imperial. The windows of the car were shut, so he couldn't call through the window ("TURN OFF ENGINE. LEAVE CAR IN NEUTRAL. CLOSE WINDOWS," said the sign above the door of the Speed Cleen Car Wash), but the car-wash attendant[1] who was crouched down vacuuming the floor behind the front seat gave no sign of hearing.

"Ashtrays, boy!" called Shreve, louder, and when the man turned his dark, blank face toward him Shreve pointed at the ashtrays. Then he closed the door and stepped back. A second attendant—a tall, skinny man wearing Army-surplus[2] clothes, a cap, and black rubber boots—was shooting steam from a hose at the wheels of the Chrysler, and Shreve, walking around the front of his car, tried to call his attention to the left headlight, which had a small mark on it—a black, V-shaped smear that looked like oil—but the man, when he looked over, merely nodded.

"Well, come on take a *look*!" called Shreve. "I'm showing you what I'm talking about." The man continued to shoot steam at the wheels, so Shreve, his face reddening, strode over and grabbed him by the arm. "Come here," he said, and led him around the front of the car. "See what I'm talking about?" he said, pointing to the mark on the rim of the light. "You see?" The man gazed evenly at it, the steam hose spitting at the ground beside him. Shreve made a rubbing motion with his free hand. "You clean that good, hear?" Then he let go of the man's arm and stepped back, shaking his head. "What's the use?" he said to himself.

Another attendant, this one in a faded sweatshirt, was attaching a small chain to the front bumper of the Chrysler; the chain was attached in turn to a thicker, heavier chain that crawled forward—gleaming with grease—along the floor of the car wash. Presently, the white Chrysler began to inch slowly into the building, following a bright-red Buick Riviera. The Buick disappeared into the steam clouds, and Shreve's car moved after it. Shreve had a last glimpse of his Alabama plate, and then a black Cadillac Eldorado was hauled by, blocking his view. Shreve watched for a moment, staring at the churning clouds, the shower of hot water, and— when the steam parted for an instant—the giant spinning brushes.

Shreve turned away and walked along the side of the building toward the front of the car wash. Beyond a chain fence was the deserted parking lot of a frozen-custard stand. "SEE YOU IN THE SPRING," said a sign on one of the big windows, but the place had a desolate, bankrupt[3] look. Across the highway was a discount furniture store. At the end of the fence, by the front of the car wash, there were several black oil drums with wringers, and men with rolled-up sleeves, breathing steam, were plunging rags into the drums, wringing them out, and then scrubbing and polishing the chrome on the newly washed cars that emerged[4] from the building. The car owners stood around, watching, waiting.

Shreve glanced into the car wash. The red Buick was just visible, covered with soapsuds, behind several other cars, but the Chrysler was still out of sight. The nearest car—a green Ford—was moving under the hot air dryer, flecks of water leaping from its roof and hood.

Shreve walked along the sidewalk, lighting a cigarette. Next to the car wash was an auto-parts store, its windows smeared with dirt; there were stacks of tires and bumpers and accessories piled in the dimness. Two hundred yards down the highway were the big blue turnpike signs. Shreve glanced at his watch. A few minutes more—five maybe—and he'd be back on the turnpike, homeward bound.

He turned back to the car wash just in time to see the red Buick emerging, gleaming in the sunlight. He strode over and peered into the building to see how his Chrysler looked. There, a few feet behind the rear of the red Buick coming slowly along on the chain, was the

[3] out of money; out of business

[4] came out

black Cadillac. Behind it was a blue Volkswagen, and behind that a gray Rover. "Where's my car?" said Shreve, almost to himself. Then he yelled, "Where's my car!"

He ran into the building. The floor was slippery with oil and water, and it was hot inside. "My car!" he yelled. "Where is it?" The faces of the attendants were blank, puzzled. He ran all the way through the building, past the unfamiliar cars, past the hot-air dryer and the hot-water rinse and the soapy brushes and the steam, and then he was outdoors again, where he had started a few minutes before. "Where is my car?" he demanded of the tall, thin man in the Army-surplus clothes. "What's the big idea?"

"What car?" said the man.

"My Imperial!" yelled Shreve. "My Chrysler Imperial!"

The man looked puzzled, and shook his head slowly. "I didn't see no Chrysler Imperial," he said.

"You cleaned it!" yelled Shreve. "I saw you clean it! I saw you clean my car!"

The man shook his head. "I don't recall no Imperial," he said.

Shreve spun around and pointed at the man with the vacuum. "You cleaned it, too," he said. "I told you 'Clean the ashtrays'! Remember—the ashtrays!"

The attendant frowned. "Don't remember no Imperial today," he said.

"But it went on the chain!" Shreve shouted. "I saw it hooked on right in front of that black Caddy. One of you must have taken it off while it was inside there."

"You can't take no car off that chain, Mister," the attendant said. "That chain's movin' all the time. It's hot in there. All that steam and stuff—you can see." He shook his head and turned slowly away, opening the door of the next car in line.

"Where's the manager?" demanded Shreve, running back inside the building. No one paid any attention. When he emerged on the front sidewalk, his clothes damp from the sprays, the men were putting final touches on the black Cadillac. Shreve grabbed a short, stout man who was polishing the rear bumper. "Where's the manager?"

"He went away for a while."

"My car's gone," said Shreve.

"You got your ticket?" asked the short man.

"What ticket?" yelled Shreve. "I didn't get any ticket!"

"Got to have a ticket," said the man. "Didn't nobody give you the ticket when you come in?"

"No!" Shreve was beginning to feel dizzy.

The short man glanced around and caught the eye of the Cadillac owner—a man in a dark suit and hat, wearing glasses. "You got *your* ticket, Mister?" he asked.

The man pulled his hand from his coat pocket and held up a small, pink ticket.

Shreve stepped over to him. "They didn't *give* me a ticket," he said.

The man turned away, shrugging slightly.

"They took my car," said Shreve.

"I don't know anything about that," said the man.

"All set, sir," said the short attendant, and the man handed him the ticket and two dollars, and got into the Cadillac, slamming the door. Shreve ran over to the car.

"Listen, friend," he said, "I'm from out of state. They—"

The window of the Cadillac rolled quietly and quickly closed, and then the car was moving away, out onto the highway. Shreve watched it drive away down the road, and then he turned back. The attendants were all busy now on the Volkswagen. No one looked at him. Shreve yelled, "I'm going to get the police, you hear? The police!"

He turned and started to stride down the sidewalk, not caring which way he was going, just getting out of there, going to find a phone. He was in front of the auto-parts store now—they might have a phone he could use—and he grabbed the door handle. It was locked. "CLOSED FOR VACATION," said a hand-lettered sign on the door. Shreve peered through the dirty window of the dark store, swearing, and he was about to turn away when he saw, on top of a heap of bumpers and tires, a single headlight—one with a small V-shaped black smear on the rim that looked like oil.

About the Author

James Stevenson was born in New York in 1929. He was a reporter and cartoonist before expanding to writing short stories for adults and picture books for children. Stevenson has said that his writing has been influenced by movies and comics. Most of his works show a wry sense of humor.

Responding to the Story

▼ Think Back

Using details from the story, explain what happened to Shreve's car.

How does Shreve treat the first two attendants?

Why didn't Shreve get a ticket? Who do you think decided not to give him one?

▼ Discuss

Why is Speed Cleen a fitting name for the car wash?

Do you think something like Mr. Shreve's experience at the Speed Cleen could really happen? Explain.

Do you feel sorry for Shreve? Why or why not?

▼ Write

Add Paragraphs As you were reading "Speed Cleen," did you have a feeling that something was going to happen to Shreve's car? Authors sometimes give clues or hints of events to come. This is called *foreshadowing*. Write two new paragraphs that you could insert into "Speed Cleen" in which you give hints about the disappearance of Harry Joe Shreve's Chrysler Imperial.

Write a Story Have you ever lost something valuable? In a short story, describe how you lost the object. Use foreshadowing to make the story more interesting.

Unfolding Bud

Naoshi Koriyama

One is amazed
By a water-lily bud
Unfolding
With each passing day,
Taking on a richer color
And new dimensions.[1]

One is not amazed,
At a first glance,
By a poem,
Which is as tight-closed
As a tiny bud.

Yet one is surprised
To see the poem
Gradually unfolding,
Revealing its rich inner self,
As one reads it
Again
And over again.

How amazing it is to watch a water-lily bud unfold! To what does the poet compare this unfolding?

[1] size and shape

Responding to the Poem

▼ Think Back

What natural event is described in the first stanza, or part, of the poem? Why does the speaker describe the event as "amazing"?

What comparison is made in the second stanza? In the third?

The first line of each stanza is similar. What purpose does the similarity serve?

▼ Discuss

Explain the two comparisons in the poem. Do you think they are effective? Why or why not?

The speaker in the poem is amazed by a small, every-day event. What everyday events amaze you? Explain.

▼ Write

Write Comparisons "Unfolding Bud" is built around a simile and a metaphor. Using the comparisons in the poem as a guide, create as many similes and metaphors as you can about objects around you.

Write a Poem Just as your understanding of a poem can deepen, so can your understanding of another person. Write a poem about how your impression of someone changed as you got to know that person better. Build your poem around a simile or a metaphor, like those in "Unfolding Bud."

Through a Glass Darkly

Bill Cosby

I wear glasses, primarily[1] so I can look for the things that I keep losing. One day, however, I did something I do not usually do: I pushed the glasses up to the top of my head when I began to read a magazine because I do not need them for reading. A few minutes later, I put the magazine down, walked out of the office in my house, and went to the kitchen for a glass of lemonade. When I returned to the office, my children were circling my desk like vultures[2] around a dying zebra.

"I would like all of you to please leave Daddy's stuff alone," I told them.

"Don't mind us, Daddy," said my little one. "We're just playing."

"And this is the one place I don't *want* you to play."

"What's this, Daddy?" she said, picking up a script she was planning to shred.

"Your next fifty meals," I replied. "Now go outside and bother your mother. That's what mothers are for."

Many of us blame others for our problems. Who does Bill Cosby blame when he loses something?

[1] mainly

[2] large birds that feed on dead animals

After they had left, I went back to my reading; but a few minutes later, I decided that I wanted to go to town for some shopping; and so, I put on my jacket, and I also wanted to put on my glasses to drive because part of safe driving is being able to see other cars.

But where *were* my glasses?

I began to look around my desk, both in and under things, wondering where my glasses had gone to hide. I checked my cigar humidor[3] and I even checked the big box containing all the things I never use and cannot throw away. The reason I cannot throw them away is simple: some day a friend may call and say, "Do you happen to have any dried-up felt markers? I can't seem to find any in the stores. And do you also happen to have a two-inch pencil with the eraser chewed off? It's my favorite kind."

With a blend of determination and dismay, I now got up and started to walk around the office. I looked like a man who was hunting for Easter eggs.

This does it, I finally thought. *There's no question about it: the kids have definitely taken my glasses. Maybe they need them for a school play. Or maybe they think I'm handsomer without them.*

I did not, however, want to go right in and yell at the kids because such anger in the past had usually triggered the reply, "Of *course* you can't find something. You always leave your stuff lying all *over* the place. The other day there was a can of *insect* spray in the fridge. It had to be yours."

[3] container to keep cigars fresh

"If people would just leave my stuff where I *put* it," I always say with partial conviction.[4]

[4] certainty

I am just like any typical nuclear physicist. My office may look messy, but I know where every atom is.

After brooding about the situation for another few minutes, I suddenly decided that the culprit was not one of my children but my *wife*, who had moved my glasses to a place in our home where they made a better blend with the color scheme. However, greater than my anger at my wife was my desire to do my shopping in town; and so, in one last desperate effort, I searched the living room, the dining room, the kitchen, and even the fuse box.

At last, I went upstairs and searched the bedroom, after which I decided to go into the bathroom for five or ten aspirin. As I entered the bathroom, I caught sight of myself in the mirror; and I also caught sight of something on top of my head: my glasses. They had been resting all this time on the great empty spaces there.

About the Author

Bill Cosby is one of the most versatile people in the entertainment industry. He has worked as a nightclub comedian, a recording artist, and a producer, as well as being the star of several television series. He has authored several books of humorous essays including *Fatherhood* and *Time Flies*.

Responding to the Essay

▼ Think Back

Why does Bill Cosby have a particularly difficult time finding his glasses this time?

Why does Cosby blame his children for hiding the glasses? Why does he blame his wife?

How would you describe Bill Cosby? What details give you clues about his personality?

▼ Discuss

Cosby states, "I'm just like any typical nuclear physicist. My office may look messy, but I know where every atom is." Do you think he knows where everything is, or is he just saying that to hide his disorganization? Explain.

Like most people, you probably misplace something once in a while. What do you think about as you search for the missing object? What usually happens?

▼ Write

Find the Humor How does Cosby describe his search for his glasses? Reread the essay. Write several paragraphs identifying the humorous parts.

Be Funny Now it's your turn. Write a short essay describing an ordinary event. Think about how Bill Cosby added humor—he used exaggeration, outlandish comparisons, and silly situations. Try to do the same things in your essay.

The Right Kind of House

Henry Slesar

The automobile that was stopping in front of Aaron Hacker's real estate office had a New York license plate. Aaron didn't need to see the white rectangle to know that its owner was new to the elm-shaded streets of Ivy Corners. It was a red convertible; there was nothing else like it in town.

The man got out of the car.

"Sally," Hacker said to the bored young lady at the only other desk. There was a paperbound book propped in her typewriter, and she was chewing something dreamily.

"Yes, Mr. Hacker?"

"Seems to be a customer. Think we oughta look busy?" He put the question mildly.

"Sure, Mr. Hacker!" She smiled brightly, removed the book, and slipped a blank sheet of paper into the machine. "What shall I type?"

"Anything, anything!" Aaron scowled.

Who would pay a fortune for a run-down house? Is it the location that makes this house so appealing?

It looked like a customer, all right. The man was heading straight for the glass door, and there was a folded newspaper in his right hand. Aaron described him later as heavy-set. Actually, he was fat. He wore a colorless suit of lightweight material, and the perspiration had soaked clean through the fabric to leave large, damp circles around his arms. He might have been fifty, but he had all his hair and it was dark and curly. The skin of his face was flushed and hot, but the narrow eyes remained clear and frosty-cold.

He came through the doorway, glanced toward the rattling sound of the office typewriter, and then nodded at Aaron.

"Mr. Hacker?"

"Yes, sir," Aaron smiled. "What can I do for you?"

The fat man waved the newspaper. "I looked you up in the real estate section."

"Yep. Take an ad every week. I use the *Times*, too, now and then. Lot of city people interested in a town like ours. Mr.—"

"Waterbury," the man said. He plucked a white cloth out of his pocket and mopped his face. "Hot today."

"Unusually hot," Aaron answered. "Doesn't often get so hot in our town. Mean temperature's around seventy-eight in the summer. We got the lake, you know. Isn't that right, Sally?" The girl was too absorbed to hear him. "Well. Won't you sit down, Mr. Waterbury?"

"Thank you." The fat man took the proffered[1] chair, and sighed. "I've been driving around. Thought I'd look the place over before I came here. Nice little town."

[1] suggested; offered

"Yes, we like it. Cigar?" He opened a box on his desk.

"No, thank you. I really don't have much time, Mr. Hacker. Suppose we get right down to business."

"Suits me, Mr. Waterbury." He looked toward the clacking noise and frowned. "*Sally!*"

"Yes, Mr. Hacker?"

"Cut out the darn racket."

"Yes, Mr. Hacker." She put her hands in her lap, and stared at the meaningless jumble of letters she had drummed on the paper.

"Now, then," Aaron said. "Was there any place in particular you were interested in, Mr. Waterbury?"

"As a matter of fact, yes. There was a house at the edge of town, across the way from an old building. Don't know what kind of building—deserted."

"Ice-house," Aaron said. "Was it a house with pillars?"

"As a matter of fact, yes. There was a house at the edge of town, across the way from an old building. Don't know what kind of building—deserted."

"Yes. That's the place. Do you have it listed? I thought I saw a 'for sale' sign, but I wasn't sure."

Aaron shook his head, and chuckled dryly. "Yep, we got it listed all right." He flipped over a loose-leaf book, and pointed to a typewritten sheet. "You won't be interested for long."

"Why not?"

He turned the book around. "Read it for yourself."

The fat man did so.

AUTHENTIC COLONIAL. 8 rooms, two baths, automatic oil furnace, large porches, trees and shrubbery. Near shopping, schools. $175,000.

"Still interested?"

The man stirred uncomfortably. "Why not? Something wrong with it?"

"Well." Aaron scratched his temple. "If you really like this town, Mr. Waterbury—I mean, if you really want to settle here, I got any number of places that'd suit you better."

"Now, just a minute!" The fat man looked indignant. "What do you call this? I'm asking you about this colonial house. You want to sell it, or don't you?"

"Do I?" Aaron chuckled. "Mister, I've had that property on my hands for five years. There's nothing I'd rather collect a commission[2] on only my luck just ain't that good."

"What do you mean?"

"I mean, you won't buy. That's what I mean. I keep the listing on my books just for the sake of old Sadie Grimes. Otherwise, I wouldn't waste the space. Believe me."

[2] a fee paid to an agent for help with a business transaction

"I don't get you."

"Then let me explain." He took out a cigar, but just to roll it in his fingers. "Old Mrs. Grimes put her place up for sale five years ago, when her son died. She gave me the job of selling it. I didn't want the job—no, sir. I told her that to her face. The old place just ain't worth the kind of money she's asking. I mean, heck! The old place ain't even worth *fifty* thousand."

The fat man swallowed. "Fifty? And she wants one-seventy-five?"

"That's right. don't ask me why. It's a real old house. Oh, I don't mean one of those solid-as-a-rock old houses. I mean *old*. Never been de-termited. Some of the beams will be going in the next couple of years. Basement's full of water half the time. Upper floor leans to the right about nine inches. And the grounds are a mess."

"Then why does she ask so much?"

Aaron shrugged. "Don't ask me. Sentiment, maybe. Been in her family since the Revolution, something like that."

The fat man studied the floor. "That's too bad," he said. "Too bad!" He looked up at Aaron, and smiled sheepishly. "And I kinda liked the place. It was—I don't know how to explain it—the *right* kind of house."

"I know what you mean. It's a friendly old place. A good buy at fifty thousand. But one-seventy-five?" He laughed. "I think I know Sadie's reasoning, though. You see, she doesn't have much money. Her son was supporting her, doing well in the city. Then he died, and she knew that it was sensible to sell. But she couldn't bring herself to part with the old place. So she put a price tag so big that *nobody* would come near it. That eased her conscience." He shook his head sadly. "It's a strange world, isn't it?"

"Yes," Waterbury said distantly.

Then he stood up. "Tell you what, Mr. Hacker. Suppose I drive out to see Mrs. Grimes? Suppose I talk to her about it, get her to change her price."

"You're fooling yourself, Mr. Waterbury. I've been trying for five years."

"Who knows? Maybe if somebody *else* tried—"

Aaron Hacker spread his palms. "Who knows, is right. It's a strange world, Mr. Waterbury. If you're willing to go to the trouble, I'll be only too happy to lend a hand."

"Good. Then I'll leave now."

"Fine! You just let me ring Sadie Grimes. I'll tell her you're on your way."

Waterbury drove slowly through the quiet streets. The shade trees that lined the avenues cast peaceful dappled shadows on the hood of the convertible. The powerful motor beneath it operated in whispers, so he could hear the fitful chirpings of the birds overhead.

He reached the home of Sadie Grimes without once passing another moving vehicle. He parked his car beside the rotted picket fence that faced the house like a row of disorderly sentries.

The lawn was a jungle of weeds and crabgrass, and the columns that rose from the front porch were entwined with creepers.

There was a hand knocker on the door. He pumped it twice.

The woman who responded was short and plump. Her white hair was vaguely purple in spots, and the lines in her face descended downward toward her small, stubborn chin. She wore a heavy wool cardigan, despite the heat.

"You must be Mr. Waterbury," she said. "Aaron Hacker said you were coming."

"Yes." The fat man smiled. "How do you do, Mrs. Grimes?"

"Well as I can expect. I suppose you want to come in?"

"Awfully hot out here." He chuckled.

"Mm. Well, come in then. I've put some lemonade in the icebox. Only don't expect me to bargain with you, Mr. Waterbury. I'm not that kind of person."

"Of course not," the man said winningly, and followed her inside.

It was dark and cool. The window shades were opaque,[3] and they had been drawn. They entered a square parlor with heavy, baroque[4] furniture shoved unimaginatively against every wall. The only color in the room was in the faded hues of the tasseled rug that lay in the center of the bare floor.

[3] blocking out all light

[4] ornately carved

The old woman headed straight for a rocker, and sat motionless, her wrinkled hands folded sternly.

"Well?" she said. "If you have anything to say, Mr. Waterbury, I suggest you say it."

The fat man cleared his throat. "Mrs. Grimes, I've just spoken with your real estate agent—"

"I know all that," she snapped. "Aaron's a fool. All the more for letting you come here with the notion of changing my mind. I'm too old for changing my mind, Mr. Waterbury."

"Er—well, I don't know if that was my intention, Mrs. Grimes. I thought we'd just talk a little."

She leaned back, and the rocker groaned. "Talk's free. Say what you like."

"Yes." He mopped his face again, and shoved the handkerchief only halfway back into his pocket. "Well, let me put it this way, Mrs. Grimes. I'm a businessman—a bachelor. I've worked for a long time, and I've made a fair amount of money. Now I'm ready to retire—preferably, somewhere quiet. I like Ivy Corners. I passed through here some years back, on my way to—er, Albany. I thought, one day, I might like to settle here."

"So?"

"So, when I drove through your town today, and saw this house—I was enthused. It just seemed—right for me."

"I like it too, Mr. Waterbury. That's why I'm asking a fair price for it."

Waterbury blinked. "Fair price? You'll have to admit, Mrs. Grimes, these days a house like this shouldn't cost more than—"

"That's enough!" the old woman cried. "I told you, Mr. Waterbury—I don't want to sit here all day and argue with you. If you won't pay my price, then we can forget all about it."

"But, Mrs. Grimes—"

"Good *day*, Mr. Waterbury!"

She stood up, indicating that he was expected to do the same.

But he didn't. "Wait a moment, Mrs. Grimes," he said, "just a moment. I know it's crazy, but—all right. I'll pay what you want."

She looked at him for a long moment. "Are you sure, Mr. Waterbury?"

"Positive! I've enough money. If that's the only way you'll have it, that's the way it'll be."

She smiled thinly. "I think that lemonade'll be cold enough. I'll bring you some—and then I'll tell you something about this house."

He was mopping his brow when she returned with the tray. He gulped at the frosty yellow beverage greedily.

"This house," she said, easing back in her rocker, "has been in my family since eighteen hundred and two. It was built some fifteen years before that. Every member of the family, except my son, Michael, was born in the bedroom upstairs. I was the only rebel," she added raffishly.[5] "I had new-fangled ideas about hospitals." Her eyes twinkled.

"I know it's not the most solid house in Ivy Corners. After I brought Michael home, there was a flood in the basement, and we never seemed to get it dry since. Aaron tells me there are termites, too, but I've

5 in a carefree way

never seen the pesky things. I love the old place, though;
you understand."

"Of course," Waterbury said.

"Michael's father died when Michael was nine.
It was hard times on us then. I did some needlework,
and my own father had left me the small annuity[6]
which supports me today. Not in very grand style, but
I manage. Michael missed his father, perhaps even more
than I. He grew up to be—well, wild is the only word
that comes to mind."

The fat man clucked, sympathetically.

"When he graduated from high school, Michael
left Ivy Corners and went to the city. Against my wishes,
make no mistake. But he was like so many young men;
full of ambition, undirected ambition. I don't know what
he did in the city. But he must have been successful—he
sent me money regularly." Her eyes clouded. "I didn't see
him for nine years."

"And," the man sighed sadly.

"Yes, it wasn't easy for me. But it was even worse
when Michael came home because, when he did, he was
in trouble."

"Oh?"

"I didn't know how bad the trouble was. He
showed up in the middle of the night, looking thinner
and older than I could have believed possible. He had
no luggage with him, only a small black suitcase. When
I tried to take it from him, he almost struck me. Struck
me—his own mother!

[6] a sum of money payable at regular intervals

"I put him to bed myself, as if he was a little boy again. I could hear him crying out during the night.

"The next day, he told me to leave the house. Just for a few hours—he wanted to do something, he said. He didn't explain what. But when I returned that evening, I noticed that the little black suitcase was gone."

The fat man's eyes widened over the lemonade glass.

"What did it mean?" he asked.

"I didn't know then. But I found out soon—too terribly soon. That night, a man came to our house. I don't even know how he got in. I first knew when I heard voices in Michael's room. I went to the door, and tried to listen, tried to find out what sort of trouble my boy was in. But I heard only shouts and threats, and then . . ."

She paused, and her shoulders sagged.

"And a shot," she continued, "a gunshot. When I went into the room, I found the bedroom window open, and the stranger gone. And Michael—he was on the floor. He was dead."

The chair creaked.

"That was five years ago," she said. "Five long years. It was a while before I realized what had happened. The police told me the story. Michael and this other man had been involved in a crime, a serious crime. They had stolen many, many thousands of dollars.

"Michael had taken that money, and run off with it, wanting to keep it all for himself. He hid it somewhere in this house—to this very day I don't know where. Then the other man came looking for my son, came to collect his share. When he found the money gone, he—he killed my boy."

She looked up. "That's when I put the house up for sale, at $175,000. I knew that, someday, my son's killer would return. Someday, he would want this house at any price. All I had to do was wait until I found the man willing to pay much too much for an old lady's house."

She rocked gently.

Waterbury put down the empty glass and licked his lips, his eyes no longer focusing, his head rolling loosely on his shoulders.

"*Ugh!*" he said. "This lemonade is bitter."

About the Author

Henry Slesar was born in Brooklyn, New York, in 1927. He is the author of more than 500 short stories published in magazines and anthologies. He has also written more than 100 television plays, including about 60 for the Alfred Hitchcock mystery series. *TV Guide* magazine called Slesar "the writer with the largest audience in America." His latest efforts include writing for the daytime serial "The Edge of Night."

Responding to the Story

▼ Think Back

According to Mr. Hacker, the real estate man, why is Sadie Grimes asking such a high price for her run-down old house? What is the *real* reason?

Why is Mr. Waterbury willing to pay such a high price for Sadie's house?

Why does the lemonade taste bitter?

▼ Discuss

In your opinion, is "The Right Kind of House" a mystery story, a revenge tale, or both? Explain.

The characters in "The Right Kind of House" are stereotypes, or flat, undeveloped characters that behave in predictable ways. What stereotypes do Aaron Hacker, Sally, and Sadie Grimes represent? Why did the author use stereotypical characters in the story?

▼ Write

Write a Plot Summary The main element of "The Right Kind of House" is its plot, which is designed to lead up to a surprise ending. Write a plot summary of the story. Include details and events that would help people who haven't read the story understand it.

Continue the Story What happened next to Sadie Grimes and Mr. Waterbury? Add another scene to the story. Make sure that it could be an extension of the original plot.

Theme Links

Surprises

In this unit, you've read stories and poems that either have surprise endings or describe situations that are not what they seem to be. You learned that you must often take a closer look before coming to conclusions about situations.

▼ Group Discussions

With a partner or in a small group, talk about the selections in this unit and how they relate to the theme and to your own lives. Use questions like the following to guide the discussion.

- Which of these selections could be considered humorous? Which are serious?
- What is surprising or interesting about the situation or event in each selection?
- Which selection surprised you the most?
- Do you enjoy stories with surprise endings more than other stories? Explain.
- Do you know of other stories or poems with surprise endings? Which ones would you recommend that someone else read?

▼ Different Endings

With a small group, review the selections in the unit. Think about how the stories and poems could be different with other surprise endings. Pick a story to role-play a different surprise ending for it. Perform your role-play for the whole class.

▼ Made for TV

Imagine that the short stories "Speed Cleen" and "The Right Kind of House" are going to be made into episodes of a mystery/suspense TV show. Choose one of the stories and design a full-page ad for a television guide. The art and the text you use in the ad should entice the reader to watch the show. Be sure to list the actors who will play the lead roles.

▼ The Theme and You

What has been the biggest surprise in your life? What happened? What did you think was going to happen? Write a personal narrative describing the surprise and how it made you feel. Describe how you feel about the incident now and what you learned from it.

Acknowledgments

Acknowledgment is gratefully made to the following publishers, authors, and agents for permission to reprint these works. Every effort has been made to determine copyright owners. In the case of any omissions, the Publisher will be pleased to make suitable acknowledgments in future editions.

Excerpt, "Clemente at Bat" from *Pride of Puerto Rico: The Life of Roberto Clemente* by Paul Robert Walker, copyright © 1988 by Harcourt Brace & Company. Reprinted by permission of the publisher.

"Fifteen," copyright © 1977 William Stafford from *Stories That Could Be True* (Harper & Row). Reprinted by permission of The Estate of William Stafford.

"On With My Life" from *On With My Life* by Patti Trull, copyright © 1983 by Patti Trull. Reprinted by permission of G. P. Putnam's Sons.

"The White Umbrella" by Gish Jen, copyright 1984 by Gish Jen. First published in the *Yale Review*. Reprinted by permission of the author.

"Freedom" from *Gifts of Age: Portraits and Essays of 32 Remarkable Women* by Charlotte Painter. Copyright © 1985. Published by Chronicle Books, San Francisco.

Excerpt, "A New Arrival," from *Life Among the Savages* by Shirley Jackson. Reprinted by permission of Farrar, Straus, & Giroux, Inc. Copyright © 1953 by Shirley Jackson, and copyright renewed © 1981 by Lawrence Hyman, Barry Hyman, Mrs. Sarah Webster, and Mrs. Joanne Schnurer.

"An Hour with Abuelo" from *An Island Like You* by Judith Ortiz Cofer. Copyright © 1995 by Judith Ortiz Cofer. Reprinted by permission of Orchard Books, New York.

"Small Song for Daddy" reprinted from *Just for Laughs* by W. D. Ehrhart, Viet Nam Generation, Inc. & Burning Cities Press, 1990, by permission of the author.

"Nicknames" from *Almost a Whole Trickster* by Gerald Vizenor. Reprinted by permission of the author.

"My Reputation" from *Days of Grace* by Arthur Ashe and Arnold Rampersad. Copyright © 1993 by Jeanne Moutoussamy-Ashe and Arnold Rampersad. Reprinted by permission of Alfred A. Knopf, Inc.

"Concha" by Mary Helen Ponce. First appeared in *Women for All Seasons: Prose and Poetry about the Transitions in Women's Lives*, May 1988. Reprinted by permission of the author.